47 Down

47 Down
The 1922 Argonaut Gold Mine Disaster

O. Henry Mace

WILEY

John Wiley & Sons, Inc.

Copyright © 2004 by O. Henry Mace. All rights reserved

Published by John Wiley & Sons, Inc., Hoboken, New Jersey
Published simultaneously in Canada

Photo credits: Courtesy Amador County Archives, pages 4, 7, 10, 18, 19, 60, 89, 91, 98, 101, 119, 139, 141, 145, 161, 163, 174, 179, 180, 193, 197, 198, 199, 201, 204, 246; Bureau of Mines, courtesy of the Amador County Archives, pages 27, 33, 35, 38, 48, 49, 51, 52, 55, 63, 70, 81, 82, 84, 85, 106, 117, 126, 128, 130, 132, 144, 150, 167, 169, 188, 189, 190, 195; Mrs. Mary Etheridge, page 99; Finney Papers, Department of Special Collections, University of California Library, Davis, CA, with permission of the Estate of Ruth Finney, pages 68, 159, 170, 249; *Stockton Record*, page 206.

Selected excerpts from the Ruth Finney Papers courtesy Department of Special Collections, University of California Library, Davis, CA, with permission of the Estate of Ruth Finney.

For general information about our other products and services, please contact our Customer Care Department within the United States at (800) 762-2974, outside the United States at (317) 572-3993 or fax (317) 572-4002.

Wiley also publishes its books in a variety of electronic formats. Some content that appears in print may not be available in electronic books. For more information about Wiley products, visit our web site at www.wiley.com.

Library of Congress Cataloging-in-Publication Data:

Mace, O. Henry.
    47 down : the 1922 Argonaut Gold Mine Disaster / O. Henry Mace.
        p. cm.
    Includes bibliographical references and index.
    ISBN 0-471-44692-0 (cloth)
    1. Argonaut Gold Mine Disaster, Jackson, Calif., 1922. 2. Mine fires—California—Jackson. 3. Gold mines and mining—California—Jackson. I. Title: Forty-seven down. II. Title.

TN423.C2M24   2004
622'.3422'0979442—dc22
                                                              2004003019

Printed in the United States of America

10 9 8 7 6 5 4 3 2 1

In memory of Ruth Finney (1898–1979),
my other red-haired muse

Contents

Preface

On a hot August day in 1995, I stood in the dilapidated hoist house of the Argonaut gold mine in Jackson, California, and was inspired to write this book. At the time I knew only the basic details of the story—forty-seven miners trapped nearly a mile beneath the earth in the summer of 1922—a highly dramatic but true chronicle of peril and tragedy that would rival any Hollywood disaster film. As I walked across the now vandalized platform on which the hoisting engineer once stood while running the controls that lowered men into the mine and brought gold ore back to the surface, it struck me that it looked very much like the derelict bridge of an abandoned sea vessel.

Working all alone in the expansive metal building surrounded by an array of knobs, dials, and switches, the hoistman must have felt a great sense of power—that he alone commanded the mine's treasure as well as the men who toiled to extract the hidden wealth from its depths. With my hand on the clutch that he once held, I realized that on the night of August 27, 1922, he must have felt like the captain of a sinking ship.

When I began my research into the Argonaut story, I could not have known that it was far wider in scope and detail than just the basic account of a mine disaster, or that it would take more than seven years to delve through the stockpile of related newspaper articles, diaries, government reports, and other resources that had survived the decades in a variety of repositories across the United States. The pieces of the story were widely scattered, but they fit together with astonishing precision.

Stories of mining disasters have always been popular because mining was and is one of the most dangerous industries in the world, and writers always seem to have a knack for romanticizing danger. Mine disasters of various magnitudes and severity were commonplace in the early part of the twentieth century, and this was especially true in the case of coal mines, which to this day hold the record for the most men killed in both individual and combined mining accidents. Primary among these was the appalling 1907 Monongah Mine disaster in Virginia, in which 362 miners perished.

Regardless of the type of mine, all underground mining work holds the same perils—explosions, rock falls, sharp edges, flying debris, and the possibility of plummeting down a shaft—but throughout the history of mining, fire has caused the greatest loss of life. Fires in metal mines (copper, silver, gold, etc.) have been far less common due to the fundamental nature of the mining process and the type of ground into which metal mines are driven. This is not to say that these mines are not dangerous. The most disastrous fire in a metal mine occurred in 1914 at the Granite Mountain copper mine, near Butte, Montana, where 163 men were burned to death or asphyxiated.

Not surprisingly, there are often similarities in the stories of miners trapped by fire. The owners of the mine almost always seem to put the value of the mine above the safety of the miners. The trapped men almost always attempt to build some sort of barricade to keep out the smoke and gas. And there is always the heart-wrenching drama of wives and families who hope against hope that *their* miner will survive.

The narrative you are about to read has all of these dramatic elements, but in the case of the Argonaut Mine disaster they are only a fraction of the story. The time—the Roaring Twenties; the place—California's historic Mother Lode; the setting—one of America's richest gold mines; and the unusual historical component of America's maturing journalism institution, with a notable female constituent, make this story unique within its genre.

When the Argonaut Mine caught fire in late August 1922, it was one of the deepest and richest gold mines in North America and one of several hundred productive gold mines that dotted California's Mother Lode region. Because the language of gold mining is essential to understanding the story of the Argonaut tragedy, my greatest challenge in writing this book was to integrate elements of the mining process into the narrative as simply and unobtrusively as possible while giving the reader the best possible *feel* for what it was like to work in a California gold mine. Ironically, many of the technical details of mine work were delved from my personal copy of Robert Peele's *Mining Engineers' Handbook*, printed and distributed in 1927 by the publisher of this book, John Wiley & Sons.

I was fortunate to have access to a wealth of material from which to extract accurate details and dialog, including the complete minutes and correspondence of the Governor's Committee on the Argonaut Mine Disaster, which came into my personal possession through an extraordinary twist of fate. However, as is always the case when telling the story of an event that occurred more than eighty years in the past, much of what was actually said by the people involved has been lost to history. The reader should know that in every case where dialog is presented, the essentials of the conversation, if not the specific words, were derived from primary source materials. We know the conversation took place, and the dialog accurately reflects the subject matter of that conversation.

While the story of the Argonaut Mine disaster has no single hero, many of those involved play a critical role in the drama. The articles and related writings of Scripps-Howard News Alliance reporter Ruth Finney play an important role in this book, as does the story of her auspicious rise to prominence as a direct result of her coverage of the Argonaut fire. Three decades after her passing, the words and the spirit of this amazing lady imparted a keen comprehension of the time and place that most surely reflects in the storytelling.

Byron Pickard, chief representative of the Bureau of Mines at the disaster, was active in every element of the story, and he developed a personal nexus with the Argonaut tragedy that lasted for decades. Pickard's highly detailed reports were all business, yet his personal thoughts and opinions could often be read between the lines.

Any accomplished fictionist would be proud to have invented a character as equally colorful and tragic as the Argonaut's venerable superintendent, V. S. Garbarini. As the man in charge, his role was one of unyielding determination marred by endless frustration.

The antagonist of the Argonaut drama is the mine itself—demanding a toll for the golden treasure that had been torn from its depths. The protagonists are the miners—forty-seven of whom were locked in a struggle to survive, while a hundred more fought valiantly to bring them out alive.

Acknowledgments

The following institutions provided access to important primary source materials and/or research assistance during the production of this book: The California State Library, California State Archives, Amador County Archives, Bancroft Library at the University of California at Berkeley, and the San Joaquin County libraries.

The families and descendants of the miners, reporters, and other primary players in the Argonaut drama, many of whom sought me out long before I knew they even existed, receive my sincere gratitude. Special thanks go to Marguerite Finney, grandniece of my numinous muse and patron of the Ruth Finney legacy.

I am grateful to my manuscript readers, Amy Lundeberg, Malisa Poujade, and Daniel Slutsky, for their honest opinions and suggestions; also to my wife, Kathryn, who provides immeasurable inspiration and encouragement through her obviously partisan praise.

I also want to express particular appreciation to the following persons and organizations for their invaluable assistance: John Skarstad, university archivist, and Daryl Morrison, Head of Special Collections, General Library, University of California at Davis; Jane DeMarchi, archivist at the U.S. Department of Labor, Mine Safety and Health Administration Library; mining artifact collectors/dealers Roger and Connie Peterson; documentary film producers Miles Saunders and Kit

Tyler; and Larry Cenotto, archivist for the County of Amador, who through dogged determination has developed what is arguably the most comprehensive and accessible small-county archives in the West.

CHAPTER 1

The Greatest Fear

Before midnight, the evening of August 27, 1922, was typically uneventful in the little mining town of Jackson, California. Colorful neon signs flashed and buzzed outside darkened stores and soda parlors. The number of cars parked along Main Street betrayed the secret of backroom speakeasies and brothels where the graveyard shift was just beginning.

Although the downtown sidewalks were quiet, the night was far from silent. An endless rumbling from no discernible source shook the streets and alleys. Store windows vibrated steadily and neon tubes hissed and jiggled in their sockets. An out-of-towner, hearing the strange, endless drone, might wonder if Jackson sat on a perpetual miniature earthquake. Locals, however, had long since blocked out the familiar grumble. It was the heartbeat of Jackson—the constant thumping of hundreds of huge mechanical hammers crushing ore at a half-dozen nearby gold mines.

On the outskirts of town, brightly lit boardinghouses teemed with activity as miners prepared for the late shift that began at 10 P.M. Others had been in the mines since 5:30 P.M. and were now looking forward to their dinner hour. On this night, four miners made their way along the dark uphill path from the boardinghouses to join forty-three others who toiled in the steamy depths of one of America's deepest and richest gold mines—the Argonaut.

At the end of a dark passageway nearly a mile beneath the surface of the earth, Luis Leon held the sledgehammer high above his head and brought it down hard against the rock. A thousand tiny slivers of white quartz shot outward from the point of impact. Caught in the glow of his headlamp, they appeared for a second like a thousand shooting stars against the blackness of the slate walls. When Luis kicked the rock with his steel-toed boot, it crumbled into a half-dozen segments. He stepped back for a moment and allowed his brother Tony to load the now manageable pieces into a nearby ore cart.

"Completo," Tony Leon said to his brother as he dropped the last fragment into the cart. "Tempo del paranzo." After five and a half hours of breaking and hauling rock, it was time for the two men to join the other miners for a dinner break.

Luis untied the shirt from around his waist and used it to wipe the streams of sweat from his face and bare chest. Then he tied it back in place and reached for the handle on the ore cart, which sat on a smooth iron plate so that it could be turned around easily and lined up with the rails on which it would ride back down the dark passageway to the mine's main shaft. Once the ore cart was in place on the rails, the brothers pushed it along with minimal effort.

As they guided the cart along the rails, Tony and Luis weren't thinking of the paltry meal that waited in their lunch boxes. In recent days their thoughts had seldom turned from the expected arrival of Luis's wife and Tony's son from Spain. Each brother had left behind a wife and children in order to make a new life in America. They expected to send for their families once enough money could be saved for the necessary boat and train passage.

As muckers in the Argonaut Mine—men whose sole purpose was to shovel and haul rock—the Leons were each paid a meager wage of $4 a day. Through careful budgeting, they had saved enough money for two tickets. Selecting the two family members who would be the first to join them in California had been a difficult decision. As they dumped the contents of the cart into the ore chute near the mine's main shaft, Luis's wife and Tony's son were aboard a steamer on the dark Atlantic en route to Ellis Island.

On this night, the Leon brothers were working 4650 feet below the surface in a horizontal passageway called a drift, which had been driven outward in search of the gold-bearing lode that often appeared as a brilliant white quartz vein in the surrounding dark green slate.

From its opening at the surface, the main shaft of the Argonaut Mine stretched 4900 feet downward into the earth at an angle of about 60 degrees, with drifts being driven outward every 150 feet or so along the depth of the shaft. Other passageways branched off the drifts—upward, downward, and outward from the sides—creating a spaghetti-like maze of underground corridors. This labyrinth was so elaborate that the mine's engineers and managers used color-coded three-dimensional maps to keep track of the ever-growing underground workings. Those who were unaccustomed to visualizing a myriad of overlapping layers of shafts and corridors in spatial aspect would find the maps perplexing and useless.

The language of mining was equally confusing to outsiders. Miners almost never used the word *tunnel*, which indicated a passageway that was open on both ends. (The Argonaut contained only one tunnel, a relatively small drainage conduit very near the surface.) The men entered the mine through a shaft, then moved into the drifts, where they extracted gold ore from

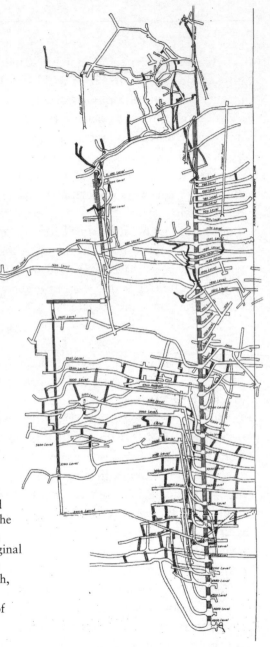

Argonaut engineers produced
large maps to keep track of the
spaghetti-like maze of shafts,
drifts, and raises. On the original
version of this map, which is
approximately 3 feet in length,
colors were used to indicate
the dimensional perspective of
overlapping passageways.

the face of the drift and from overhead stopes that had been driven up into the ceiling of the drift. As the stope was driven higher, wooden chutes were installed just above the drift to hold the ore in place until it could be dumped directly into waiting ore carts.

A stope that was driven continually upward until it broke through the floor of the drift above was renamed a raise. A raise might also be driven upward with the sole purpose of connecting two drifts. Additional passageways, driven outward through the wall of a drift in search of gold ore, were called crosscuts, and in some cases, these had several branches.

The rock wall at the end of a drift or crosscut was called the face. Most rock taken from the face of a drift while it was being driven had no significant gold content and was therefore called waste rock. The sinking of shafts and the driving of drifts was called development work, as distinguished from mining work, which involved the extraction of gold-bearing ore.

For the Leons and the other miners, each day in the mine was a mirror of the previous. At the face of a drift, or up in a stope, drillers used heavy jackhammers with rotating bits to bore strategically placed holes in the rock. Then blasters filled the holes with dynamite and detonated the charges, relying on gravity to do the work of extracting the chunks of gold ore that fell to the floor of the drift. Muckers broke the rock into manageable pieces and loaded it into carts, then hauled it out to the main shaft and dumped it into another chute.

The entrance to each drift was a large room called a station that opened into the mine's main shaft. The various drifts were also known as levels, and both the levels and their stations were named for their distance in feet from the surface.

The tools and explosives used in the mining process, as well as the massive wooden timbers that were required to support the walls and ceilings of the drifts and crosscuts, were stored in the respective stations. Immediately below each station was an ore chute, accessible through iron doors on the station floor. Gold ore or waste rock brought out from the drift was dumped into this chute and held there until it could be hauled to the surface. Periodically the chute was emptied into a skip (each ore skip typically carried over 4 tons of rock) and the material was hauled to the surface, where, under the direction of the mine's "top man," it was carried high into the headframe and automatically dumped, once again taking advantage of gravity to facilitate loading the material into ore carts.

The worthless waste rock produced through development work was trammed out to a dump pile, and the valuable gold ore obtained through the mining process was conveyed to the mill, where massive hammers, called stamps, crushed the ore into a fine powder that had the consistency of talc. A steady stream of water carried these fine particles over a series of copper plates painted with mercury. Like a magnet, the mercury drew out the fine grains of gold, and the remaining sludge, called tailings, was expelled into a flume that carried it to a holding pond. (In the early days of deep rock mining, this soupy mixture of finely crushed ore and water was washed into nearby streams and eventually made its way into California's fertile Central Valley, choking the streams and rivers and contaminating agricultural lands. In 1915, the mining companies in northern California signed an agreement with valley farmers and ranchers that required each mine to impound their tailings in a holding pond on their own property.)

At regular intervals throughout the day, a group of five stamps, called a battery, was shut down so that the mercury, which was now an amalgam with the gold, could be scraped from the plates and carried to the processing plant. Through a distillation process called retorting, the mercury was boiled off and recovered. At the end of the process, the bottom of the

A rare panoramic composite of the Argonaut 3900 station and the entrance to the 3900 drift. Because the miners' eyes were fully dilated in the intense darkness, they appear almost cartoon-like in the instant illumination of the photoflash.

retort held a craggy mass of nearly pure gold that looked like a golden sponge. Later, this would be melted into bars and shipped to the U.S. Mint in San Francisco.

Working in the stamp mill was no less dangerous than working in the mine—the perils were just of a different nature. It was not uncommon for crew members toiling near the booming stamps to be struck deaf within a year. Those who constantly handled mercury and breathed its fumes ultimately fell victim to quicksilver poisoning.

All of this dangerous and elaborate processing was required because the raw ore that was extracted from the Argonaut Mine was of extremely low grade. The price of gold had been set by the government at $22 per ounce, and the typical value of ore from the Argonaut was $70 per ton, which meant that each ton of processed ore yielded a little over 3 ounces of gold.

While this seems a minuscule return for so much effort, the cost of mining and milling seldom exceeded $5 per ton, and the Argonaut processed over 100,000 tons of ore in 1921 alone. From 1893 to 1930, the Argonaut mill would extract nearly

800,000 ounces of gold through the nonstop mining and milling process.

It was the job of those who trammed the ore to collect samples from each cart that would later be fired and assayed to determine the grade of the ore. But because the ore was of such low grade and the milling process occurred far away from the working levels of the mine, the typical miner never saw more than a speck of the yellow metal he worked so hard to retrieve. On those rare occasions when high-grade gold was found underground, the excitement level was high and the temptation was strong.

A myriad of schemes had been devised to pilfer high-grade ore—a process logically called highgrading. A large pocket watch with the works removed could carry an ounce or more, if the miner had time to pound out and flatten the gold. The use of various body cavities was perhaps the most uncomfortable alternative but also the quickest and most effective. One miner was known to keep a string tied to his tooth so that he could attach the other end to a small chunk of high-grade ore, swallow it, and retrieve it once he had left the mine property. There were more than a few shady characters in town who would buy high-grade ore, no questions asked, for less than 50 percent of its actual value.

The managers of the Argonaut Mine knew that a relatively small percentage of their gold would be highgraded, and like most mining companies, they had a standing offer to buy back high-grade ore from brokers—at a substantial discount, of course, and with no questions asked. Miners who were caught in the act of highgrading, however, were immediately dismissed and might find themselves blacklisted from working at other mines.

At 10:00 P.M. on the evening of August 27, 1922, skip tender Steve Pasalich waited patiently in the stark, bare-bulb lighting of the Argonaut Mine headframe as the four late-shift miners boarded the skip. This large metal bucket with a heavy iron bail was used to transport men and equipment into the mine and hoist men and rock back to the surface. The Argonaut was served by two separate skips that ran up and down the inclined shaft on metal rails. Each of these skips was attached to more than a mile of 2-inch-thick cable that was reeled up and down through the control of hoistman Thomas Brewer. Pasalich was sort of an elevator operator who rode on the bail of the skip. Using an electrically powered bell system that could be activated at any station or from the skip itself, he could signal the hoistman to raise or lower the skip as required.

The hoist house, with its enormous electric motors and two giant hoisting wheels, sat several hundred feet downhill from the entrance to the mine. The hoisting cables ran from the hoisting wheels, through a large hole in the wall of the hoist house, then several hundred feet uphill to the top of the mine's massive headframe that towered over the shaft, and finally downward to the skips below.

The Argonaut shaft was divided into three compartments, each measuring 4 by 5 feet. Two of these narrowly accommodated each of the skips, and one compartment, called a manway, contained a ladder, water pipes, and telephone and electric wires. Only the stations and sections of the main shaft were lit by electric lighting. From the shaft's main opening, called the collar, to the lowest level of the mine, called the sump, the shaft walls were supported by sets of large wooden timbers that held the fragile slate walls in place.

With the four miners secured inside the bucket, Pasalich swung himself onto the bail and pushed the signal button— three rings, then two rings. At the hoist house, Brewer recognized this sequence of bells as the standard signal to lower a skip with men aboard. He released the brake on the hoisting reel and threw the clutch that would set it in motion. Pasalich

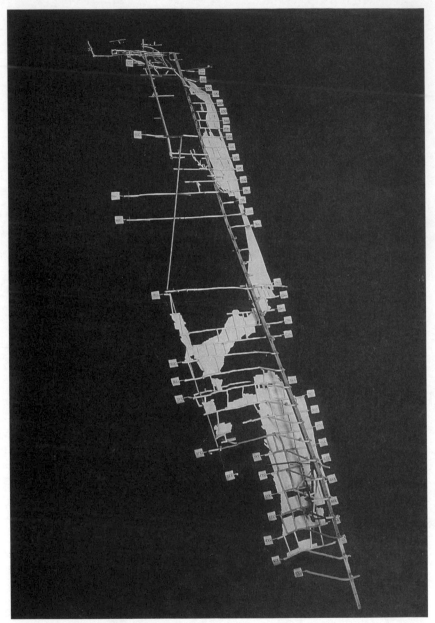

Made of wire and sheet metal, this tactile 3-D model of the Argonaut Mine was originally created to be used as an exhibit in a lawsuit.

quickly moved to the center of the bail and took a firm hold. The skip eased away from the collar, slowly at first, then faster. The five men found themselves in familiar darkness for a short period, then a dim glow surrounded the bucket as it approached the first station. The light grew brighter, the station flashed by, and the light quickly dimmed. One hundred fifty feet later, another station, another flash of light—this one came quicker.

The skip was soon descending at a speed of nearly 700 feet per minute. Stations flashed by every four or five seconds, and from inside the bucket the miners kept track of the levels by counting the flashes of light. With each passing station, the air became warmer and more humid, and the miners' breathing became more labored. An acrid metallic odor filled their nostrils. The skip began to slow down as it passed the 4650 station, where the two Leon brothers were dumping ore into the chute. When they saw Pasalich on the bail, one of them shouted, "How long to lunch?"

The skip had already dropped below the station when Pasalich shouted back in his thick Slavic accent, "I go back up for buckets now!"

When the skip reached the 4800 level, the hoisting mechanism stopped, but the bucket continued past the station for several feet, then bobbed up and down a few times before settling level with the station floor. At this depth, the mile-long cable reacted much like a massive rubber band, expanding and contracting according to the weight of the load.

Without speaking, the four miners stepped out onto the station floor and unhooked the carbide lamps from their hats. They filled the lamps with powdered carbide and water, then lit the flame that would guide them back into the working area of the drift where electric lines had not yet been strung.

Carbide lamps operated through an ingenious but relatively simple concept. The base of the lamp was a small can divided into two compartments. The top compartment held water and the bottom held calcium carbide in tablet or powdered form. When the water dripped down onto the carbide, the resulting chemical reaction produced acetylene gas forced out through a nozzle on the front of the lamp. In much the same manner that modern cigarette lighters are lit, the gas was ignited by flicking a small flint-and-steel wheel mechanism attached to a reflector surrounding the nozzle. The lamp was then hung from a metal tab that was riveted to the front of the miner's soft cotton cap. The size and intensity of the flame was controlled by adjusting a mechanism that regulated the frequency of the drips of water.

Before the introduction of carbide lamps, miners used ordinary wax candles to light their way underground. The classic miner's candlestick, of forged iron, could be hooked onto the front of a miner's hat, stuck into a wooden beam, or even jammed into a crack in the rock to provide close-up lighting. More than a few underground fires were started by the careless use of candles, and even though their use was prohibited by most mining companies in the early part of the twentieth century, many veteran miners still used them in the 1920s.

Although the carbide lamp was much safer and far more practical than the standard wax candle it supplanted, its use presented a new array of problems and dangers, especially in wet mines like the Argonaut. If a miner dropped an open can of carbide on a wet floor in a confined space, he would soon be surrounded by explosive acetylene gas. And since three of every five miners were seldom seen, above or below ground, without a cigarette drooping from their lips, a source of ignition was almost always present.

Every element of a miner's work included a degree of danger. The labor was backbreaking and treacherous. Blasters—those men who positioned and detonated the dynamite—were the most likely to be injured or killed. But every man who worked in the mine was in peril from falling down the shaft or being struck by falling rock. The skip, plunging downward at high speed, was only inches away from timbers that could remove a hand or a head in a split second of carelessness. The first hard hats, covered in durable tortoiseshell, were still a decade in the future.

When asked to describe the extraordinary underground world of a California gold mine, most miners would say you had to be there to understand it. With colorful and dramatic hyperbole characteristic of '20s-style journalism, San Francisco attorney and freelance writer Andrew Perovich gave readers a brief but fervent glimpse into the miner's privileged realm in an article for the *San Francisco Call:*

> There is a certain overpowering sense of being cut off from everything you read about, everything you hear about in experience and everything you feel down here.
>
> This is a world set apart—and there comes a certain overpowering shaft from some subconscious plane of human emotion that we have died and are reborn in another world, and possess another body—a strange bone-bulging body which we do not recognize.
>
> You are down in the bowels of the oldest thing this side of chaos—earth. And there is a certain shivery feeling you get when crawling into a hole. The nerves of your back shake, your shoulders hunch, and it seems as if the very walls and roof are closing in on you.
>
> Every minute you expect to find tons of earth crumbling and crashing down upon that space between your shoulder blades. The very thought seems to smother, and you find yourself panting.

Of all the perils he faced, day in and day out, a miner's greatest fear was an underground fire. Like so many others before him, his life might come to an end under a pile of fallen rock, or he might slip and fall down the shaft, or he might even be decapitated by a shaft timber if he carelessly stuck his head too far outside a moving skip. But that was the death of one man, gone in an instant. A mine fire could kill dozens of men, and often it was a terrifying and agonizingly slow death.

Beyond a respectful attention to the rules of safety, the miners usually gave little thought to the dangers of their profession. On this night, however, several of the Argonaut miners had expressed uneasiness about going to work. As his wife prepared his lunch, miner George Steinman told her, "Something is going to happen." When she pressed him about it, he laughed it off and left for his shift at the mine.

Earlier in the evening, miner Emanuel Olobardi and his wife, Amelia, attended a banquet held by the Italian Benevolent Society. When they returned home, Amelia noticed that her husband's mood had turned somber. "We've had such good times," he said to her, "that I fear something awful is about to happen. I don't like to go back to work, but . . . I guess it's all a foolish notion."

Emanuel was one of the four miners who had just arrived at the 4800 station of the Argonaut Mine. There were now forty-seven men working in the lower levels.

CHAPTER 2

Like the Frames
of a Motion Picture

As Steve Pasalich watched the four miners disappear into the darkness of the 4800 drift, he signaled the hoistman to pull him back to the surface. The cable creaked and groaned above him, and the skip began its ascent. In less than ten minutes, Pasalich was at the collar of the shaft, loading the miners' lunch buckets in the south skip.

At 10:40 P.M., he rang the skip down to the 1600 level and passed out buckets to two men—the only miners working in the upper levels of the mine. Then he continued downward toward the 4000 level so that he could check the condition of an ore chute at that station. At about the 2000 level, Pasalich passed three miners who had just gotten off shift and were being hoisted out of the mine in the north skip. The two skips shot past each other so quickly that there was no time to exchange greetings.

After inspecting the 4000 chute, Pasalich climbed back on the bail and signaled the hoistman to continue his descent.

Nothing happened. The skip set stationary for several minutes. Finally, Pasalich hopped off and picked up the station telephone.

"Brewer," the hoistman answered.

"What the matter?" Pasalich asked. "Why go keep me here?"

"Something's wrong with the rope," Brewer replied. "Wait just a minute and I'll let the skip down."

Pasalich stepped back onto the bail and waited patiently for five more minutes before the skip started moving downward. He stopped the skip again at the 4500, 4650, and 4800 levels, where he passed out buckets to miners who had gathered at those stations.

Great care was taken by management to assure that workers could not secretly remove high-grade gold ore from the mine, and this included inspecting and securing all lunch buckets. When the miners arrived for work, they entered a change house where they removed their street clothes in one room, then put on work clothing in an adjoining room. The men walked naked through a connecting hallway so that absolutely nothing could be transferred between the two rooms. Lunch buckets were deposited with an inspector and held in security until they were delivered by the skip tender at the appropriate time. The inspection process would be reversed at the end of the shift.

By 11 P.M., Pasalich had delivered all of the buckets, and the men were enjoying a short respite from their hard labor. Most of the miners were emigrants from Southern Europe—Italians, Spaniards, and Serbians, among others. During the dinner break, those with a common ethnicity usually sought each other out, and their boisterous conversations melded into a strange babble that echoed into the drifts and up the main shaft. For a few minutes, the stench of the dank station was surmounted by the subtle combined aromas of foreign spices, rich teas, and strong coffee.

Many of these men, like the Leons, were striving to bring relatives to America. Some of them had been separated from their families for several years. Working an average of twenty-five days each month, they took home a paycheck of about $100 after deductions for clothing and lost or damaged equipment. A room in a boardinghouse cost $10 a month, without meals. For men living with families, a one-room shack would run at least twice that much. A set of work clothes, consisting of denim pants, shirt, and jumper, also cost $10. Miner's steel-toed boots were $8 a pair. Coffee was 30 cents a pound and vegetables were 12 cents a can. A new Ford automobile cost four-month's wages.

The mine operated twenty-four hours a day, 365 days a year, and there was no limitation on the number of hours a man was allowed to work, as long as he performed his duties diligently. Some of the forty-seven miners working in the Argonaut Mine on the night of August 27, 1922, had not taken a day off in twenty-one days.

In 1922, the Argonaut was the second richest single mine in the state. She would produce more than $25 million in gold before all of the gold mines in California were closed by executive order in 1942.

The richest single gold mine in California at the time was the Argonaut's nearby neighbor, the Kennedy Mine, which would take out a total of $34 million during its productive lifetime. (The Empire Mine, in Grass Valley, California, has long been publicized as the state's richest gold mine, but the total production figure of $130 million is an aggregate of several neighboring mines that had been consolidated under a single mining company.)

In all, a quarter-billion dollars in gold would be extracted from the depths of the Mother Lode—a 120-mile-long gold-bearing geological formation that stretches from Georgetown in the north to Mariposa in the south. These mines varied from

The Argonaut Mine, Jackson, California: 1. headframe; 2. mill; 3. Muldoon shaft; 4. hoist house; 5. waste dump; 6. water tower.

one-man operations using hand-cranked hoists to large corporate ventures utilizing the latest mining technology and employing several hundred men in a variety of positions.

The Argonaut and Kennedy mines were both discovered in the early 1850s—the former by two African-American freedmen, William Tudor and James Hager, and the latter by Irish immigrant Andrew Kennedy and his partners. The two mines operated with modest success until each was acquired by separate corporate entities in the latter part of the nineteenth century.

The paths of the two competing mines would cross, quite literally, in the summer of 1894, when lawyers for the Argonaut Mine Company filed suit against the Kennedy for trespassing into the gold-bearing vein beneath the Argonaut property. The court case centered around a complicated and often vague 1873

An overview of the Argonaut (1) and Kennedy (2) mines shows the relative proximity of the two properties.

mining law that had always been open to interpretation. Arguments involving extralateral rights, vein apex, and parallel property end lines would drag on for five years before a California circuit judge would finally rule in favor of the Argonaut. This was the first in a long series of litigations initiated by both mines over the next fifty years that would feed a seemingly endless and bitter rivalry.

By 1922, the Argonaut had reached a depth of 4900 feet and the Kennedy was down below 4000. The exact depth of the Kennedy at any given period in time is difficult to determine because the management of the Kennedy Mine was particularly secretive about development details. This cautious approach was no doubt born of the competitive nature of the business, as well as the ongoing conflicts with their litigious neighbor. All of this secretiveness was rather moot, since miners were constantly leaving one mine to work for the other, bringing some knowledge of the competition's progress with them.

The underground depth of the two mines was specified in linear distance downward from the collar of the shaft. Therefore, the level designations of the fully vertical Kennedy shaft did not match the level designations of the inclined shaft of the Argonaut. Also, the Argonaut sat on a hill above the Kennedy. Taking all of these factors into consideration, the 4900-foot level of the Argonaut Mine matched up approximately with the 4000-foot level of the Kennedy. Adding to the confusion, those involved in mining had a tendency to round off or abbreviate level numbers—for example, referring to the 4350-foot level of a mine as "the 4300" or even just "the 43."

Except for variations dictated by the angle of their shafts, operations in the two mines were carried on in a similar manner. As time passed, shafts were driven deeper, new drifts were driven out into the gold-bearing lode, and ore was extracted and milled.

The process of milling gold ore involved great amounts of water, much of which came from the mine itself. For the most part, both the Argonaut and the Kennedy were wet mines—the Kennedy somewhat more so than the Argonaut because of its lower depth in relation to sea level. The miners' clothing, shoes, and socks were always soaked through. Groundwater constantly dripped from the ceilings and seeped from the walls. It drained through ditches along the edge of the drift, then down the main shaft to the sump at the bottom of the mine. From there, it was pumped up to the surface and distributed as needed.

More than 72,000 gallons of water were pumped from the mine during each twenty-four-hour period. This water contained significant amounts of arsenic and other dangerous by-products of the mining process. Once it passed through the mill, deadly mercury was added to the list of contaminants.

Unlike naturally formed caves, which are generally quite cool even at significant depths, the temperature in a gold mine typically increases 1 degree F with each 40 to 100 feet of depth.

This warming is due to natural geothermal conditions deep below the earth's crust. A miner might have gone to work on a winter's night when the outside temperature was below freezing, and later find himself working in an unventilated drift nearly a mile below the surface where the temperature exceeded 100 degrees F.

At the end of the day, the miners returned to the change house and placed their wet, dirty clothes on a peg in a heated compartment that was intended to dry them out before the next shift, although the system often failed in this regard. Laundry was done only once each week, and by week's end, a strong, musty, sour odor accompanied the miners everywhere. The stench was especially noticeable when twelve or more men crowded into the bottom of a skip for the brief ride in or out of the mine.

During daylight hours, the Argonaut Mine had a full complement of management personnel on duty, including the mine manager and his assistant, and a host of foremen and assistant foremen. But during the late night hours, when most of the work was being performed underground, the shift boss was in full command of the men and their labor.

On each working level of the mine, a miner designated the level boss made sure that the shift boss's wishes were carried out to the letter. One or more of these men might be designated the jigger-boss, a mostly honorary title for an experienced miner who acted as sort of an assistant to the shift boss.

On the night of August 27, 1922, shift boss Clarence Bradshaw was in charge of the mine and the men. His duties involved anything and everything required to keep the mine running efficiently including pitching in himself wherever needed. Whereas a standard miner received a daily wage, Bradshaw received a monthly salary—a paycheck nearly twice that of the men he supervised.

On this Sunday night, Bradshaw came on shift at 6 P.M. and spent the first four hours making his way through the active levels of the mine, confirming that the crews were all in place and had been informed of their assignments. On the 4650 level, he talked with level boss Charles O'Berg about his duties for the night. Charles was working for the first time with his son, Arthur. Earlier in the week, he had asked for a schedule change so that he and Arthur could work together during Charles's last year at the Argonaut. He planned to retire the following year.

After talking with the O'Bergs, Bradshaw moved down to the 4800 level to check in with Ernie Miller, the only jigger-boss on duty that evening, who was working that level with his partner, Niko Stanicich. Miller had many years of mining experience and had proven to be a reliable overseer.

As the dinner break approached, Bradshaw was back on the 4650, helping Charles O'Berg and his son run an ore cart out to the chute. They arrived at the station just as Pasalich began passing out lunch buckets to the men.

Bradshaw sat on a stack of timbers and unpacked his dinner from the two compartments of his miner's lunch pail. His wife had placed boiled potatoes and a slice of ham in the center section, and an apple and some loose tea in the bottom of the bucket. Bradshaw removed the center tray, retrieved the apple from the bottom, then unscrewed the tin cup that was attached to the top of the lid. One of the other miners passed him a dipper of fresh water, which he poured onto the tea leaves in the bottom of his pail. He then put the center tray back in place, lit his carbide lamp and placed it on the floor, then held the bucket above it for a few minutes. The already tepid water quickly began to boil, brewing the tea and warming the ham and potatoes.

Bradshaw had just poured his tea into the tin cup when Steve Pasalich and Mitchell Jogo, the skip tender's helper, approached him.

"What I have to do tonight?" Pasalich asked. "Chutes all full on top and waste chute full on 33."

"Draw the waste on 33 and lower it to the 4200 chute," Bradshaw answered.

"That chute full also," Pasalich said.

"Okay. Wait until I get through with my supper. I'll go up and run that chute and you two boys can go with me," Bradshaw responded.

The three sat and conversed for a few minutes while Bradshaw gulped down his meal.

"Okay, what time you got?" he asked as he reassembled his lunch bucket.

Pasalich pulled out his pocket watch. "Twenty-five past eleven."

"Let's go to it," Bradshaw said.

The three men climbed aboard a skip and Pasalich rang it to the 4200 level.

Fifty feet back into the 4200 drift, Bradshaw, Jogo, and Pasalich rolled an ore cart under an overhead chute and prepared to pull out the stop board, a heavy wooden plank that acted as a door for the chute. As Pasalich began to pull the board away, the falling rock ripped it from its bracing and buried it under several hundred pounds of debris. Before the now fully loaded ore cart could be moved, a new stop board had to be put in place. Jogo volunteered to take a skip down to the 4600 level where the lumber and saws were stored and cut a replacement board. After taking a measurement of the opening, Jogo left for the station. Bradshaw and Pasalich continued to work in the crosscut.

When ten minutes had passed and Jogo had not returned, Bradshaw became impatient. "How long does it take for that guy to cut a damn board?" he grumbled.

After waiting a couple more minutes, the two men became impatient and started walking back down the drift toward the main shaft. As the 4200 station came into view, Pasalich noticed that everything looked hazy. Then the stinging odor of burning timbers reached his nostrils.

"My God, Brad," he shouted. "There's a fire!"

Bradshaw quickly stepped out onto the manway ladder from the 4200 station and stared upward into the smoke-filled shaft. His eyes strained to penetrate the gray haze, searching for a glow that might indicate the location of a fire. Because the angle of the shaft was inconsistent, he could see only a few hundred feet above him. With neither of the two skips available at the station, he decided to climb the ladder in order to gain a better view.

Several hundred feet below, Jogo finished cutting the replacement stop board for the 4200 ore chute and was walking back to the skip when he heard Pasalich's voice echoing down the shaft.

"Jogo, bring skip up now!" Pasalich shouted excitedly.

As Jogo climbed aboard the skip, he got the first whiff of smoke. He signaled the hoistman to pull him up, and as the 4200 station came into view, he could see Pasalich pacing anxiously.

"Fire someplace in shaft!" Pasalich shouted as he jumped onto the bail of the skip, not waiting for it to come to a stop.

"Where Bradshaw?" Jogo asked as he tossed the stop board out onto the station floor.

"He take ladder to climb up," Pasalich replied as he gave the signal to start the skip moving slowly upward.

Bradshaw had climbed nearly to the next level when he heard the approaching skip. He carefully crossed over to the middle compartment and jumped onto the bail as it drew near.

By the time the skip reached the 3900 station, the three men were coughing uncontrollably as they held their hands over their nose and mouth in an effort to filter the thick smoke and fumes. Pasalich rang the skip to a stop and Bradshaw quickly ran to the station telephone to call the hoistman.

"Tom, there's a fire! On the next signal, pull quick!" he ordered. Then he jumped back onto the skip and rang the signal bell.

As the skip sped upward, the three men huddled in the bottom of the bucket, still attempting to filter out the smoke with their hands. Just below the 3000 level, they passed through the fire. Braving the intense heat and using the sleeve of his shirt to help filter the smoke, Pasalich stood and peered over the edge of the bucket. Flames were burning fiercely in the manway compartment over a distance of about 10 feet. The heat was intense and the smoke burned his eyes and throat. Coughing and gagging violently, Pasalich fell backward into the skip.

"I'm almost in," he gasped.

Suddenly, the smoke cleared and fresh air poured down onto the three groggy miners who were now clinging to each other in the bottom of the skip. Jogo dragged himself up to the bail and gave the signal to stop. They were at the 3000 level, some 20 feet above the flames. As Bradshaw and Pasalich stumbled out onto the station floor, Jogo climbed over from the skip to the manway ladder and stared down at the fire. The smoke appeared to boil as it rolled upward for a few feet, then was drawn back downward. The air in the 3000 station was clear and fresh—the mine's forceful ventilation system was pulling both the smoke and the fire down the shaft toward the unsuspecting miners below.

During the Argonaut's early years, engineers had designed a ventilation system that incorporated the underground workings of a nearby abandoned mine called the Muldoon. As drifts were driven out from the Argonaut main shaft, fresh air circulation was maintained by connecting each drift with the old neighboring shaft. A massive exhaust fan had been installed at the collar of the Muldoon that pulled air down the Argonaut shaft, through the workings, then back up the Muldoon. When the depth of the Argonaut exceeded that of the Muldoon, new drifts were connected to the circulation system by driving a raise upward to the drift. When work was discontinued on a particular level, a ventilation door was installed that closed off circulation and forced fresh air down to the lower working areas. There was no need to install a latch on these doors; the powerful suction of the Muldoon fan kept them tightly sealed.

The Muldoon shaft also served to legally satisfy the Bureau of Mines requirement for an alternative emergency exit. However, the hoisting system in the Muldoon Mine only operated to a depth of 950 feet. Below that, a confusing labyrinth of connecting tunnels and raises zigzagged their way nearly a mile up from the mine's working levels.

Ironically, hand-lettered signs strategically placed to direct miners through the maze were written only in English, even though 75 percent of the mine's personnel were foreign immigrants. Although portions of the route were inspected annually, no miner working in the Argonaut's lower levels had ever attempted to exit the mine through this web of remote passageways.

While all of the mines were typically strict about work schedules, they permitted a certain amount of flexibility on Sundays. Miners who wanted to pick up some extra hours could volunteer for Sunday work. Those who wanted time off could easily be excused from a Sunday shift.

At the Argonaut Mine, a typical weeknight shift was comprised of seventy-five men, but Sunday night was always a light

The collar of the Muldoon shaft. The Argonaut exhaust fan sits below small headframe at left.

shift. On the night of Sunday, August 27, 1922, twelve miners were absent because they had requested time off to go hunting. Several men were on vacation. On this night, the total underground complement of forty-seven workers was one of the lowest ever for any shift at the Argonaut Mine.

As midnight approached, two muckers returned from running an ore cart out to the 4800 station and informed jiggerboss Ernie Miller that the lunch buckets had not yet been picked up. As Miller approached the station, he was fully prepared to see an army of rats scurrying over the buckets, lured as usual by the small morsels of food left inside.

Mostly blind from living in near-perpetual darkness, the mine's rat population had developed an amplified sense of smell and were attracted to even the slightest crumb of food. Other than an occasional "thinning" of the population, the rats were tolerated by mine workers, as on ships at sea, as a sign of safety.

To Ernie's surprise, when he arrived at the station there was not a single rat to be seen. He reached for the telephone to call the top man, then suddenly stopped and took in a deep breath of the stale mine air. A shiver ran down his spine and the hair on his arms tingled. He smelled a frighteningly familiar odor that brought back a horrible nightmare. It unfolded in his mind like the frames of a motion picture.

It was the night of June 8, 1917. Ernie Miller was one of 410 men working in the Granite Mountain copper mine in Butte, Montana, when a fire broke out above them, on the 2400 level. The mine's ventilation system quickly pulled smoke down onto the men below. While some of the miners crowded into skips and were hoisted to the surface, those left behind sought refuge from the ever-increasing carbon monoxide gas.

Out of the chaos and confusion, Ernie stepped forward as a leader. He organized his coworkers and hurried them into a crosscut where the smoke had not yet penetrated. He enlisted the cool heads among the miners to help him build a barrier against the dangerous carbon monoxide that might soon lure them into a deadly sleep. The miners stacked timbers and chinked the cracks with mud, then sat down to await fate's verdict: death or rescue. For four days, they prayed, they sang, they talked. Then came the glorious sound of picks tearing away at the bulkhead and the flashing headlamps of a dozen miners helping them out of their tomb. Out and up to fresh air and freedom; to nourishing food, clean water, and the safe arms of a loving family.

One hundred sixty-three Granite Mountain miners would not be so lucky. It took two weeks to bring all of the bodies out of the mine. Many were so badly decomposed that they could not be identified.

Now, five years later and even deeper below the surface of the earth, memories of that nightmare seemed more vivid than ever. Ernie Miller moved cautiously to the edge of the station and looked upward into the hazy blackness.

The smell of burning timbers was now strong and unmistakable.

His next thought was half prayer, half silent shout.

Please God, not again.

CHAPTER 3

Their Worst Enemy

From his viewpoint above the fire, Jogo could see how quickly the flames were spreading and realized that time was of the essence if there was to be any chance of getting the miners out.

"Do something, quick!" he shouted across to the two men standing on the station.

Both Bradshaw and Pasalich were still gasping for air. "What are we going to do?" Bradshaw asked. "She's got an awful start and we have nothing to fight it with."

Pasalich tried to shake off the effects of the smoke and heat. "We go to 2000. Some water tanks there, I think."

The two men boarded the skip and rang it to the 2000 station, leaving Jogo hanging from the manway ladder. When the logic of this action was later questioned, Bradshaw would explain that he thought Jogo had said, "Go quick," and assumed he wanted them to go on without him.

As the skip started upward, Pasalich looked down on the glowing fire and shook his head somberly.

"Shaft gone. . . . Boys gone. . . ."

At the 4800 station, Ernie Miller lifted the earpiece on the telephone and turned the crank that would send a signal to all of the other phones in the system. The number of times the phone bell rang indicated who the call was intended for. The hoistman answered one ring; the top man answered two.

"One bell?" asked an excited voice on the other end.

"Yes," Ernie replied. "There's smoke coming down the shaft."

"All right." Ernie now recognized Thomas Brewer's voice. "Wait a second. Bradshaw will be on the line. Brad— . . . someone on the line wants you. Talk to him first."

"Bradshaw, . . ." Ernie interjected. "There's smoke coming down the shaft."

"Yes, the shaft is on fire and we are going to try to put it out," Bradshaw hurriedly replied.

Momentarily stunned by Bradshaw's matter-of-fact answer, Ernie replied, "All right," and hung up the phone.

For Ernie Miller, this was all too familiar. He knew from experience that the actions he took in the next few minutes could mean life or death for the miners working in the three lower levels of the mine. With smoke now choking his lungs, he rushed back into the drift and gathered his crew, then directed them up the manway ladder to the 4500 station. He sent several men into the 4650 drift to collect the workers on that level and bring them up to the 4500 station as well.

Miller knew that time was quickly running out. He led the assemblage through the 4500 drift, picking up the miners assigned to that level along the way. His options were limited. His first hope was to take the men out through the ventilation raises on the Muldoon side, but before they reached the 4500 ventilation door, the smoke and fumes had become nearly unbearable. The miners quickly retraced their steps back to a long crosscut off the main passageway. The smoke had herded the men into an unventilated dead end raise, but it too was quickly filling with carbon monoxide.

As Bradshaw hung up the phone at the 2000 station, he became even more agitated and bewildered. Hearing Miller's concerned voice from below reminded him that lives were at stake and underscored the need for urgency. He and Pasalich had stopped at the 2000 station to search for firefighting equipment and to telephone Brewer to ask him to call the mine foreman. Pasalich had found some old fire extinguishers at the station but was unable to make them function and eventually tossed them aside.

The tenseness of the situation and the residual effects of carbon monoxide wore heavily on Pasalich's physical condition. His tongue was now dry and swollen, and he was having trouble swallowing. Frustrated by their inability to find anything with which to fight the fire, Pasalich and Bradshaw again climbed aboard the skip and rang it to the collar of the shaft. As they moved toward the surface, Pasalich slumped over the bail. "I'm done in, Brad," he muttered. "Done in."

At the collar of the shaft, the two men stumbled from the skip and ran to a nearby water bucket, where they gulped down water from a tin dipper and dumped several dippers full over their heads.

Bert Turner, the top man for the late shift, had not yet been advised of the fire and was surprised by the haggard appearance and excited demeanor of the two men.

"What's the matter?" he asked.

"There's a fire in the shaft." Bradshaw forced the words out between deep breaths. "Did anyone send word to Ben?"

"I don't know. No one told me about a fire," Turner answered.

Bradshaw turned and staggered toward the mine office several hundred feet down the hill from the headframe. Halfway there, he saw the mine foreman, Ben Sanguinetti, coming up from the nearby parking lot.

"Hurry up!" Bradshaw shouted to him.

"Where exactly is the fire?" Sanguinetti asked as the two men strode quickly toward the collar of the shaft.

"Just below 3000."

Argonaut Mine foreman
Benjamin Sanguinetti.

"Let's get the skips filled with water."

"They won't hold it. Too many holes."

"Okay. Find every keg or can that will hold water."

Sanguinetti grabbed a mining cap and carbide lamp from the change room, then picked up the telephone to call Brewer at the hoist house. He lifted the earpiece from its cradle and turned the crank. No bell rang—no one answered. He tried again—still silence.

From his ladder perch 3000 feet below the surface, Jogo continued to watch the flames lick at the dry timbers. All he could think of was the men below. Why didn't someone send the skips back down for them? He could see the skip rails clearly in the glow of the fire. The Argonaut main shaft was supported by sets of timbering, each set about 5 feet square. The fire was burning across two sets in the manway portion of the shaft and was still confined mostly to the upper portion or roof—what miners called the hanging wall. Jogo was sure that skips could still make it through if they hurried.

Frustrated at not being able to do anything, Jogo clung helplessly to the rungs of the ladder, watching and waiting. Suddenly, the electric lights on the station flickered out. He spun his head around. The station was faintly lit by the light of his carbide lamp but only for a brief moment. Then it too began to dim. His lamp had run out of carbide.

He was now engulfed in darkness, except for a smoky glow from the flames below. Until that moment, he had not thought about the danger of being so close to the raging fire and so far from the safety of the surface. His heart began to pound as he scrambled up the manway ladder.

At the hoist house, Brewer anxiously awaited further instructions. The last information he had received was that they were going to attempt to fight the fire, but he was too far from the collar of the shaft to see what was happening and it seemed forever since he had received any signals.

During normal operations, Brewer kept the two skips operating in balance—as one skip came up, the other went down. But when he was notified of the fire, he quickly realized that both skips would be needed in the firefighting efforts, so he disengaged the balance of the hoisting system and brought both buckets to the collar of the shaft.

With the skips sitting stationary at the surface and both of the electric hoisting motors sitting idle, the hoist house was eerily quiet. Brewer listened intently, waiting for the signal bells to vibrate their instructions—or for that single ring that would tell him that someone wanted him on the phone. Suddenly, every bell in the building began to ring. Both the telephone and skip

Argonaut hoistman
Thomas Brewer standing
by the two hoisting reels
used to raise and lower
the two Argonaut skips.

signal bells emitted one long, steady clatter, then abruptly went silent. Brewer picked up the phone and yelled, "One ring?" No one answered. He turned the crank twice to signal the top man. No bell rang; no one answered.

He stepped down from the hoisting control platform and walked outside the building. His eyes strained against the darkness as he stared up the hill toward the Argonaut headframe. Then he saw a bright lantern being swung back and forth. The light stopped swinging and moved across to the collar of the shaft, where it shone brightly on one of the supporting timbers for the headframe. He quickly realized that it was illuminating the support where the telephone was mounted.

Brewer ran back into the hoist house and picked up the phone. "Hello!" he shouted.

"Hello, Tom. This is Ben. The fire has shorted out the bells and I'm going to need you to lower us exactly like this. . . . Wait one minute after I hang up, then lower the north skip slowly to the 2400. I'm going down the ladders from there. Hold the skip at the 2400 for thirty minutes, then pull her up. Got that?"

Brewer repeated the instructions back to him.

"Be sure and lower us slowly. I have no idea how far the fire has progressed and we may need to jump off," Sanguinetti explained.

One minute later, Sanguinetti, Bradshaw, and Pasalich were aboard the skip with a dozen cans of water as it slowly sank into the dark Argonaut shaft. At the 2100 level, they passed Jogo, who had been climbing the manway ladder for nearly twenty minutes. The light of three carbide lamps danced on his concerned face as the three men moved slowly past him in the skip.

"What are you doing there?" Sanguinetti shouted. Bradshaw and Pasalich had failed to mention that they left Jogo at the 3000 station.

"Climbed up," he shouted back matter-of-factly.

"Well, climb back down to 24 and follow us," Sanguinetti yelled.

At intervals of approximately 300 feet along the depth of the shaft, the Argonaut electricians had installed switches so that if they needed to work on the electrical system below a certain level, they could cut off power at that point, leaving the rest of the system in operation. From the 2400 station, Sanguinetti dropped down the ladder to the 2600 and pulled one of those switches, restoring the phone and signal bell service above that level. He continued down the ladder to the 2800. The fire was entirely obscured by smoke, which was now rising nearly 100 feet before being pulled back down the shaft.

"I imagine it was 75 or 80 feet below the 28," Sanguinetti later recalled. "I saw it was useless to send any skips through. You could hear timber fall. The pump column was buckling and boiling. It would have been useless to send the skip down."

Sanguinetti scanned the shaft below him, trying to make a careful assessment of the conditions. A large pipe, called the pump column, which brought drainage up from the sump at the bottom of the mine, was trembling as the water inside it boiled. Suddenly, a seam on the pipe split and steam began to spew out. Then the pipe burst wide open and a rush of steam rolled upward. Sanguinetti began to scramble up the manway ladder, but as he looked over his shoulder, he could see that the mine's ventilation system was still performing its function. The steam rose only a few yards above the smoke before it was pulled back down the shaft and disappeared with a hiss into the flames.

With the bells back in working order, Pasalich was able to ring the skip down to the 2800 level and retrieve Sanguinetti. All four men then rode back up to the 2000 station, and Sanguinetti picked up the telephone receiver, intending to call the surface. A familiar voice was already on the line.

"Mr. Garbarini," the foreman cut in. "This is Ben, at the 2000 station."

As superintendent of the Argonaut Mine, Virgilio Garbarini had the reputation of a seasoned, no-nonsense mining professional. Like many of the men in his charge, Garbarini was first-generation Italian-American. His parents came to Jackson when he was only five years old, and although he didn't do particularly well in school, he did show a strong aptitude for drawing and problem solving. By age 22, he was working in the local mines, where he learned mechanical engineering mostly by osmosis. In subsequent years, he was employed by seven different

Virgilio S. Garbarini, superintendent of the Argonaut Mine.

mines along the Mother Lode, often as an independent contractor. By 1905, when he was elected to serve as the first mayor of the city of Jackson, Garbarini was a recognized expert in the fields of mining mechanics and bridge construction.

In 1909, Garbarini was hired by the Argonaut Mine as a master mechanic. The Argonaut's hoisting system, headframe, stamp mill, and tramway were all designed by Garbarini and built under his supervision. He accepted a position as mine superintendent (also known as the mine manager) in January of 1921.

In addition to his desk at the Argonaut main office, Garbarini maintained a small office in a separate building behind his home, just south of Jackson. He often worked late into the night and liked the solitude of his private sanctuary. He did not expect to be called to dinner until everything was on the table and ready to eat. His wife, Katie, and his nine children kept silent throughout the meal. "Better for the digestion," he told them.

While he demanded quiet and solitude at home, he never failed to speak up and let his own opinion be known in discussions, whether domestic, civil, or corporate in nature. There was no room in his world for small talk or laziness. Nor could he tolerate failure. Challenges were to be met and conquered.

When Garbarini arrived at the Argonaut Mine shortly after midnight, he asked the top man where Sanguinetti and the other men had gone. Turner told him they had gone down to fight the fire, then asked if he should go down to the Muldoon shaft and stop the ventilation fan.

"No, don't touch the fan!" Garbarini barked. "You have men in the shaft now trying to put the fire out. If you stop that fan, you will reverse conditions and crowd the boys out of the shaft, and they won't be in position to get to the fire. Leave things alone until you hear from me. Be sure not to touch *anything* unless you hear from me."

Like Garbarini, mine foreman Ben Sanguinetti was a longtime employee of the Argonaut and an experienced mining man. Unlike his boss, he was easygoing and amiable, willing to obey orders without question, and ready to defend the decisions of his superiors.

Without having discussed the situation, Sanguinetti and Garbarini were already on the same page. They needed to put out the fire and save the mine—and, consequently, save the lives of the forty-seven men below.

"What are you doing at 2000?" Garbarini asked his foreman on the phone.

"We're at the sump reservoir. I want your permission to turn it down the shaft onto the fire," Sanguinetti said.

"Yes, of course. Turn her down," Garbarini replied.

Sanguinetti already had a wrench in place on the valve. He gave it a strong tug. The valve wouldn't budge. Pasalich put his hands over the top of Sanguinetti's and the two men pulled together. The valve was unyielding. Sanguinetti grabbed a sledgehammer and smashed it against the handle of the wrench. There was still no movement.

The drain valve on the sump reservoir had not been opened since the sump pump had been installed many years earlier. Because of the power limitations of sump pumps, water from the bottom of the mine could only be pumped to the 3900 level. It was held in a tank there from which a second pump sent it to the 2000 tank, and a third pump sent it to the surface. Before the 2000-level pump was installed, water was taken out of the mine by draining it from the 2000 reservoir into a watertight skip and hoisting it out. Opening the valve on the 2000 reservoir would cause the water to shoot out into the shaft hopefully with enough force to reach the manway compartment where the fire raged.

Sanguinetti picked up the phone and again called the superintendent on the surface. "Mr. Garbarini? The valve won't budge. We've tried everything we have down here."

"Murphy's coming down with the water skip," replied Garbarini. "I'll send some better tools with him."

During the first thirty minutes after his arrival at the mine that night, Garbarini had designed a mechanism that would allow a skip filled with water to be emptied through a small trap door at the bottom. He then directed the Argonaut assistant foreman, Lloyd "Doc" Murphy, and two other employees to weld the piece in place. Murphy ordered the skip filled with water and rode the bail down into the mine.

When he arrived at the 2000 station, Murphy also tried his hand at the sump valve, to no avail. Communicating by telephone, Garbarini ordered the men to break it open. They beat at the valve mercilessly with heavy sledgehammers. Bent and battered, it remained solidly in place.

Garbarini was furious. "Send up a skip," he ordered. "I'm coming down there."

Pasalich turned to Sanguinetti. "I go up. Can't stand no more. Legs gone, and head, it pound."

"I'll go with you," said Bradshaw. "We'll take the north skip." When the two men reached the surface, Bradshaw decided to go home. He would never return to the Argonaut property.

Five minutes later, Garbarini was standing at the sump tank on the 2000 station wielding a sledgehammer. He ran his hand along the pipe in back of the valve, searching for a seam, then stepped back and gave the pipe a sharp blow from the bottom. The seam popped open and a long stream of water gushed out into the shaft.

Garbarini tossed the sledgehammer on the station floor. "Now, let's get this water skip down there and see what good we did."

This time, they could only go as far as the 2700 station. The fire had advanced over several more sets of timbers. The water from the reservoir never made it to the flames—it simply ran down the footwall of the shaft. And while Garbarini's makeshift release worked perfectly, the force of the water from the skip was also insufficient to reach the flames. It was clear that the fire had progressed far beyond any possibility of fighting it with the methods they had devised.

Sanguinetti called the hoist house. "Get us out of here, Tom. We need to replace this skip with a water tank and hose."

"Ben, should I try to send the other skip down for the men?" Brewer asked.

"It's too late" was Sanguinetti's sober reply.

* * *

Shortly after midnight on the morning of August 28, in a dark, smoke-filled crosscut off the 4350 drift, the miners of the Argonaut night shift listened to Ernie Miller's plan. The ventilation system that had once kept them alive was now their worst enemy. The mine was quickly filling with poisonous gas. Even if they could find their way through the Muldoon escape route, carbon monoxide poisoning would overtake them long before they completed the mile-long climb to the surface.

The men knew that Miller had been in a similar situation and survived, and they trusted his guidance. The use of a bulkhead to keep out the smoke and carbon monoxide had worked at Granite Mountain, but they needed to find a refuge from the flow of smoky air. As they made their way down the 4350 crosscut, the choking odor of burning timbers moved with them. There would be no time for second guessing. They would make their stand here.

Along the route, the miners collected loose wood—discarded dynamite boxes, broken boards, and bits of timbering. Several feet back into the crosscut, they found mounds of waste rock that had been left behind when this section of the mine was abandoned. Working as a team and driven by the will to survive, they began to build a barrier to shut out the smoke. Timbers were wedged into position and lagging was placed across them. Rock was carefully stacked against the lagging until it reached the ceiling. When the smoke continued to seep through, the men removed their jumpers, shirts, and socks. They tore them into strips, soaked them in mud, and chinked the cracks.

Hot, tired, nearly naked, and drowsy from the effects of carbon monoxide, the miners were not ready to say they had done their all. There was still plenty of loose rock left. They moved back 25 feet farther into the crosscut and began a second bulkhead.

CHAPTER 4

A Meeting of Minds

3 A.M. Monday, August 28—Day 1

When the ringing telephone awoke him from a deep slumber and he saw no light streaming through the bedroom window, U.S. Bureau of Mines district engineer Byron Pickard knew he was in for a long day. He shook the cobwebs from his head and listened intently to the voice on the other end of the line. George Downing, assistant manager of the Argonaut Mine, was telling him there was a fire in the main shaft and perhaps as many as seventy-five miners were trapped on the lower levels of the mine. Pickard informed him that the resources of the bureau would be made available and that he would set the necessary wheels in motion.

From its inception in 1910, the primary purpose of the Bureau of Mines, as defined by Congress, was to improve mine safety by educating mine employees and by conducting research on the causes and prevention of mine accidents. Even though the bureau's scope was widened in 1913, it wielded no actual authority to dictate or enforce mine safety regulations. By 1922, the Bureau of Mines had established a chain of mine safety stations near active mining districts. These were sometimes affiliated with a mining school or college, as was the case with the mine safety station of the University of California at Berkeley.

As part of their educational objective, the bureau also equipped and maintained a number of mine rescue cars. These specially designed railroad cars were outfitted with the latest rescue equipment and were staffed with a fully trained crew, including a foreman miner, first-aid miner, engineer, physician, clerk, and cook. These rescue cars traveled to mining towns throughout the district, providing safety instruction to miners and mine managers. In cases of actual mine emergencies, one or more rescue cars were sent to the nearest railroad terminal and the crew was supplemented by rescue teams from the local safety station. Minutes after getting the call from the Argonaut Mine, Byron Pickard telephoned Rodney Hecox, foreman miner of the Berkeley Safety Station.

"We've got a bad one, Rod. Fire at 3000 in the Argonaut has trapped the whole night shift. Downing says it's out of control and already burned through telephone and electric wires. I need you to get the crew together and meet me at the station. I'll call McDonald."

B. F. McDonald, the station's first aid miner, was waiting in front of his Berkeley home when Pickard arrived in the bureau's new Dodge truck. On their way to the bureau's Berkeley facilities, they stopped at a Western Union office so that Pickard could send a telegraph to the safety station at Elko, Nevada, requesting that Mine Rescue Car #1 be dispatched to the Central Pacific Railroad terminus at the town of Ione. Then the crew and equipment would need to be transferred to the Amador Central Railroad's narrow gauge cars before continuing on to the town of Martell, which was located less than a mile from the Argonaut Mine.

At the Berkeley Safety Station, Hecox and Pickard supervised the assembly and loading of breathing apparatus and rescue equipment onto two trucks. Hecox and McDonald started for Jackson in the first truck at 5 A.M. Pickard waited for the arrival of the bureau's district surgeon, C. E. Kindall, and the two men left with the second truck at 6:30 A.M. The 140-mile drive to Jackson would take five hours. As the dry plains of the Sacramento Valley gave way to the undulating foothills of the Sierra Nevada, a distant cloud of gray smoke in the clear blue August sky marked their final destination.

By dawn, word of the Argonaut fire had spread throughout the county and the area around the collar of the Argonaut shaft was awash in a sea of onlookers. Employees, volunteers from other mines, relatives of the trapped miners, and curious spectators milled around the collar of the shaft and perched on anything that was high enough to serve as an overlook. Throughout the night, Garbarini and his crews had dumped thousands of gallons of water down the shaft in an effort to extinguish the flames. This endeavor continued to be their focus, even though it had become obvious that the water was not reaching the fire.

Argonaut crews were quickly learning that fighting a fire in the narrow confines of the Argonaut shaft was dangerous and ill-advised. The superintendent's own brother nearly fell to his death when overcome by carbon monoxide.

John Garbarini later told reporters about his experience:

> I got a little too much gas. I guess my own bad judgment was to blame. I got down the shaft about 15 feet below a water skip. When they opened the valve and shot the volume of water, it sent the gas up along the sides of the shaft in one great wave. We had made our way clear below the 2700-foot level and it was getting very hot. We had no masks, and we were 100 feet below telephone communications. I had noticed little puffs of gas and once or twice had felt a little weak in the knees.

Just before the water fell, I foresaw the danger and tried to shout across to my brother, the superintendent, who was on the other side of the shaft, but there were all kinds of noise and he did not hear.

I heard the water hiss on the flames below. At the same instant, I felt an overpowering wave of gas. Immediately, I started to climb the ladder. My feet were very heavy and my legs and hands were numb. I held my mouth and nose shut with one hand and hooked the other around a signal wire, feeling my hand become paralyzed as I did so. It was simply a question of whether or not I could climb up through that gas cloud before I would again have to breathe. I made it about 5 feet and then I was aware that my nephew, Earl, was climbing down the ladder above me. He tried to reach down to me just as I weakened and was nearly torn from the ladder.

I was almost unconscious but began to feel pure air. Somehow I had the strength to climb about 50 feet with Earl's help and that of my brother, who had managed to get across the shaft. He had been partly gassed himself. Suddenly I became totally unconscious. I knew I had fallen. He told me later that I had fallen forward over the lip of the 2700-foot level, where Earl was able to hold me until both men pulled me up.

The foreman of Amador County's Central Rescue Station, Bob Duncan, had been on the Argonaut property since 2 A.M., but neither he nor his crew members were allowed to participate in firefighting or rescue operations. Duncan had raised Garbarini's ire by asking the question that many had already put to the superintendent: Why had the Muldoon fan not been stopped? Garbarini gave a cursory reply and told Duncan he would let him know when his services were needed. At 4 A.M., without Garbarini's permission, Duncan led a group of men on an exploratory expedition into the Muldoon shaft. When they reached the 2400 level, they were turned back by a thick wall of smoke.

In order to protect themselves from the smoke and gas, Duncan and his men wore Gibbs Self-Contained Breathing Apparatus, the forerunner to modern SCUBA diving gear. Invented by a mining engineer in 1915 and manufactured by Edison Laboratories after 1918, the Gibbs apparatus looked very much like a twenty-first–century astronaut's backpack. Utilizing an ingenious system of tubes, valves, and breathing bags, it permitted oxygen from a small tank to be inhaled through a mouthpiece. Exhaled air was directed down a tube to a regenerator that contained carbon dioxide absorbent, then recirculated back to the mouthpiece. Thus, by cleaning and recycling exhaled air, the Gibbs device could provide more than two hours of breathing time from a small 270-liter oxygen bottle.

The Gibbs apparatus was emblazoned with the word *permissible* in large capital letters, making it immediately recognizable as one of only three breathing devices approved by the Bureau of Mines for mine rescue work. All of California's mine rescue stations were equipped with this apparatus and provided with operational training. The most obvious drawback of this device in mine rescue work was its limited operating time. Ironically, the bureau would later learn that a new breathing apparatus known as the Paul device, with a four-hour limit, was available at the time of the Argonaut fire.

With a full oxygen tank, the gear weighed a cumbersome 35 pounds. Learning to safely operate the multitude of valves and controls required several weeks of training, the most important element of which was panic control. The interruption of airflow due to a pinched hose or errantly adjusted valve was a common occurrence, requiring the wearer to calmly hold his breath and make the adjustments required to restart the flow of oxygen.

One of several apparatus teams active in firefighting and rescue efforts at the Argonaut Mine.

Those trained in the use of the Gibbs device were logically called apparatus men, and in addition to the backpack, these men were issued an important yet very basic piece of supplementary equipment—a canary in a small wooden cage. Although gas detection and analysis technology did exist in the 1920s, nothing was deemed more reliable in determining underground survivability than observing the reaction of a caged canary—a practice that had been in use for more than a century. Canaries reacted to carbon monoxide in a manner almost identical to humans. If the bird was in distress, a human would be similarly distressed. If the bird died, it was a sure sign that a human could not survive if exposed to the same conditions for more than a few minutes.

Local safety stations held monthly meetings that included training in the proper use of breathing apparatus. Large mines such as the Argonaut were supposed to send at least two men to each meeting, although there was no penalty for not comply-

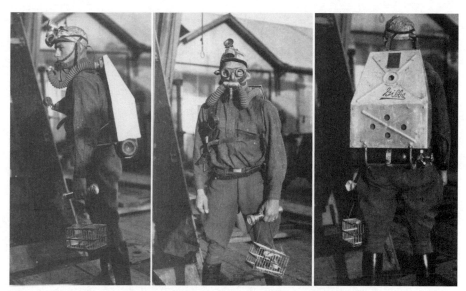

Three views of Lt. Lee F. Post of the 91st Air Squadron, Crissy Field, San Francisco, wearing the Gibbs self-contained breathing apparatus. Post carries a battery-powered flashlight and a caged canary used to determine survivability in gaseous atmospheres.

ing with this recommendation. During the year prior to the fire, miners from the Argonaut had attended just two of the twelve scheduled meetings.

10 A.M., Monday, August 28—Day 1

When Rodney Hecox arrived at the Argonaut, he immediately sought out the mine superintendent so that he could offer the services of the bureau's rescue equipment. Once again, Garbarini's response was that he would let them know when he needed help. The befuddled Hecox then went in search of someone who could give him a better idea of the situation. After a few minutes of conversation with Bob Duncan, Hecox better understood what he was up against. Before anyone from the outside was going to be allowed to lend a hand, they would have to convince V. S. Garbarini that they could offer something of value. Duncan and Hecox decided to leave that unpleasant task to the more experienced and diplomatic Byron Pickard, who was expected to arrive early that afternoon. In the meantime, the two men would establish a temporary rescue station and set about preparing the bureau's breathing apparatus and other rescue equipment.

Pickard and McDonald arrived at about 1 P.M., almost at the same time as mining engineer Fred Lowell of the Industrial Accident Commission (IAC). Unlike the Bureau of Mines, the scope of the IAC included far more than mines and mining. But like the bureau, they lacked any specific power to institute and enforce regulations. The IAC's primary function was to assist in rescue and recovery, investigate the cause of accidents, report their findings, and make recommendations. Because of their specialized knowledge and experience, members of the IAC were invaluable as consultants and advisers.

After getting an update from Hecox and Duncan and learning of Garbarini's reluctance to allow any outside help, Pickard and Lowell also tried to arrange a meeting with the Argonaut superintendent. Once again, Garbarini advised them that he was not interested in their help. With some gentle prodding, Pickard convinced him to sit down with them and discuss the possibilities.

In the small shack that served as the office of the Argonaut Mining Company, Pickard, Garbarini, and Lowell examined a three-dimensional model of the mine's underground workings and reviewed the situation. The fire had started in the manway portion of the shaft just below the 3000-foot level of the mine and quickly spread to both skip compartments. It was believed that forty-five or forty-six men were trapped underground. At the time the fire was discovered, those men had just finished their dinner break at stations on the 4500-, 4650-, and 4800-foot levels of the mine. No attempt had been made to send the

From left to right: Fred Lowell, Industrial Accident Commission district mining engineer; Byron O. Pickard, Bureau of Mines district mining engineer; Ernest A. Stent, vice president, Argonaut Mining Co.; Peter Accher, Argonaut Mine day-shift boss.

skips back down to the trapped men because the fire quickly made the shaft impassable.

No rescue could be attempted through the Muldoon shaft because it was filled with smoke and carbon monoxide, and no available breathing equipment would allow sufficient time for rescuers to climb down such a great distance.

Pickard again asked the enduring question that would be debated among mining men for years to come: Since the exhaust fan in the Muldoon shaft was pulling the smoke and carbon monoxide down on the trapped men, why wasn't that fan turned off—or, better yet, why not reverse it and push fresh air down in the opposite direction? Pickard later recalled:

> Garbarini explained that the fan could not be reversed inside of four or five hours, as when the fan had been

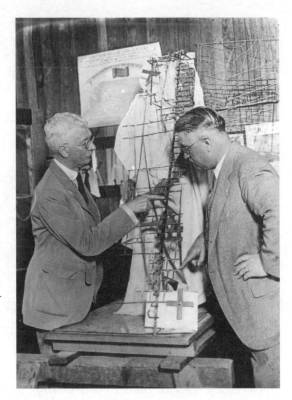

Argonaut vice president Stent and Kennedy president Hutchinson examine the 3-D model of the Argonaut underground levels.

installed no arrangements had been made for reversal of air current. [He] was also positive that reversing the fan would in no way affect the fire, as the air would be short-circuited through the doors in levels above the fire zone. It was also barely possible, he stated, that the men would be getting a supply of fresh air from the Kennedy workings and had taken refuge in the 4200 crosscut on the Kennedy side where there had always been a leakage of fresh air. If they had succeeded in reaching these fresh air currents, reversing the flow of air would force the foul gasses in on them and cut off the chance of escape. The question of reversing the air current was discussed at length with the mine model to illustrate whatever ideas and plans were brought up.

Without the downward pull of the ventilation system, the fire would logically burn upward and with greater rapidity. Within a mater of hours, the entire shaft above 3000 feet would surely be destroyed and could even collapse, leaving no practical means of entry into the mine. Both Pickard and Lowell argued that the upward draft caused by the burning fire could, in fact, quickly draw the smoke and carbon monoxide out of the mine, perhaps saving the men from asphyxiation and making a rescue attempt through the Muldoon shaft far more feasible.

Garbarini once again reminded them that this upward draft would only affect those connecting drifts in the upper part of the mine. Ventilation doors on those levels were being held closed by the suction of the Muldoon fan. If the fan was shut off or reversed, the doors would pop open and circumvent the flow of fresh air to the lower levels of the mine.

In the face of overwhelming opposing logic, it was a testament to Garbarini's reputation in the mining community that he was able to convince both Pickard and Lowell that reversal of the fan would do more harm than good. A number of other proposals were placed on the table. Each time, Garbarini shot them down with logical and seemingly valid rationale. Soon, he had convinced Pickard and Lowell that fighting the fire—a course of action that had been a failing proposition for more than twelve hours—was the most reasonable plan.

6 P.M., Monday, August 28—Day 1

Late Monday afternoon, the superintendent of safety of the Industrial Accident Commission, Hugh Wolfin, arrived at the Jackson airport. (The 122-mile trip from San Francisco's Crissy Field to Jackson in a De Haviland airplane with Lt. Lee Post at the controls was made in a record time of fifty-eight min-utes.) After earlier telephone conversations with Pickard, Wolfin had decided that the Argonaut might obtain valuable assis-tance from the neighboring Kennedy Mine if he could get the two mining giants to put aside their longstanding differences. When he walked into the office of the Kennedy Mining and Milling Company, he was surprised to be greeted by the com-pany's president, E. C. Hutchinson, who had been in Jackson since Saturday night on his monthly visit to the mine. Wolfin was even more surprised with the generous offer Hutchinson proposed.

Prior to 1920, the Kennedy and Argonaut were connected on several levels where operations at the two mines had met head-on. In March 1919, a fire started in the Argonaut Mine that smoldered for several months, eventually spreading to the Kennedy through a connecting drift. It was finally decided that the only way to extinguish the fire was to flood both mines. After the mines were dewatered, all of the connecting drifts were sealed so that fire would never again be able to spread from one mine to the other. Hutchinson was now offering to reopen one of these drifts so that a rescue of the trapped Argo-naut miners could be attempted.

As the sun set on a laborious and unproductive day of fire-fighting, Garbarini, Pickard, Wolfin, and a host of important mining men attended a meeting at the Kennedy Mine office— an impressive hilltop three-story Italian colonnade that over-looked the mine's main yard. This may well have been the first time representatives of the two mines had met anywhere other than a courtroom. In fact, on this very day, as Hutchinson was offering to disrupt operations at the Kennedy and dedicate his crews to a rescue operation, lawyers for both mines had battled in court over damages caused by the 1919 fire and flood.

For half a decade, the Argonaut and Kennedy mines had made every effort to keep their rival neighbors from seeing

54

The Kennedy's sprawling stamp mill and towering headframe dominate this view of the mine property.

maps of their underground workings. Now the maps lay beside each other on the table. Ironically, both maps had been surveyed and produced by the same man, civil engineer W. E. Downs. The task of choosing which connecting drift should be opened and how the work should be done now fell on Downs's shoulders.

A comparison of maps indicated that the end of the Kennedy 3150 drift was closest to the Argonaut workings. Only 5 feet of greenstone separated the two mines on that level when the drift was sealed off during the 1919 fire. A connection at this point, however, would break through near the 3600 level of the Argonaut, which was now within the lower limits of the fire zone. After conferring with engineers from both mines, Downs mapped out a plan to reconnect the previously closed Kennedy 3600 drift with a crosscut near the Argonaut 4200

station, where V. S. Garbarini believed the men may have barricaded themselves.

The project of connecting the two mines would not be a
simple one. Over 1400 feet of the abandoned Kennedy 3600
drift would be badly caved in due partly to the effects of the
flooding but also due to natural compression. When mining
operations cease and underground workings are abandoned,
especially at a depth of more than 1,000 feet, nature makes
every attempt to reclaim the ground. As supporting timbers rot
away, the walls and ceiling of the drift begin to collapse from
intense pressure. Water backs up in drainage ditches and fills
the drift with sludge. In some cases, shifting ground causes the
floor of the drift to heave up within inches of the ceiling. All of
these problems were expected in reopening the Kennedy 3600
drift.

In addition to clearing out the old drift, Downs decided
that the rescue miners would also need to drive two totally new
passageways in virgin ground in order to make the connection
as quickly as possible—the first, a crosscut to bypass a long U-
shaped curve in the old drift; the second, a diagonal raise to be
driven upward from the end of the drift in order to connect
with the floor of the Argonaut 4200 crosscut. Gold mining
operations at the Kennedy Mine would be discontinued for the
time required to complete the connection and effect a rescue of
the Argonaut miners. Mining teams for the project would be
selected from volunteers from both mines. Argonaut crews
would work under the direction of Argonaut assistant foreman
Doc Murphy. Kennedy crews would be directed by Kennedy
mine foreman Bill Sinclair. Estimates of the time required to
reopen the drift varied, but many believed it would take no
more than four days.

While the majority of the mining experts who attended this
meeting agreed with the decision, it was not without its detrac-
tors. Ben Hoxie, superintendent of the Fremont gold mine, was

adamantly opposed to the plan. After reviewing the same information given to Downs, the thirty-year mining veteran appealed to the gathering.

"You can't possibly get through in less than two weeks—very likely three weeks," he told them. "The only way to save life is through the Muldoon shaft."

Hoxie believed the best way to reach the miners was to shut off the Muldoon fan, which would cause a reversal of the airflow through the naturally upcast Argonaut shaft. (The higher of two connected shafts is always naturally upcast.) As smoke began to clear from the Muldoon shaft, Hoxie would immediately send down crews to prop open ventilation doors on the successive levels of the mine. This would reduce the possibility of smoke and gas being forced back on the miners, should they be barricaded on the 4200 as Garbarini suspected. At a point below the fire, after fresh air had replaced the smoke and gas, rescuers would eventually be able to move across a connecting drift and down the Argonaut shaft. Hoxie estimated it would take less than a day to clear the mine of smoke and locate the trapped miners.

With Argonaut superintendent Garbarini leading the naysayers, nearly everyone at the conference opposed Hoxie's plan. After the meeting, on the porch of the Kennedy office building, he was approached by his friend, E. H. Higgins, a mining consultant.

"Hoxie, they're all against you. You must be wrong," Higgins told him.

"One time there was a man called Columbus who thought the world was round and everybody else thought it was flat," Hoxie replied. "Columbus was right, and I consider that, when it comes to this question, I am Columbus. My plan is sound. The plan they came up with in there is doomed to fail."

CHAPTER 5

The Cream
of the Crop

The morning of August 28, 1922, was the busiest of Mary Cook's career. As chief operator for Pacific Telephone in Jackson, operation of the switchboard during the graveyard shift often fell on her shoulders. Shortly after midnight, Mary put through an urgent call to the Argonaut Mine foreman, Ben Sanguinetti, from the mine's hoist operator, Thomas Brewer. At the request of Sanguinetti, she then called the mine manager and his assistant, as well as the foreman of the local safety station, informing them that a fire had been discovered in the mine. Mary then took up an unofficial role as community newscaster. Among the first to be contacted was the *Stockton Record*'s bureau manager, Pearl Wright.

When her phone rang in the early morning hours, Pearl's first thought was that there was a family emergency. Newsworthy events just didn't happen in Jackson at three in the morning, and even if something did happen overnight, few people would know about it until the next day. She listened intently to the operator and her heart sank. As she quickly dressed and grabbed her notebook and pencil, she hoped that the story would be over by the time she reached the mine.

During her long uphill walk to the Argonaut Mine, it never occurred to Pearl that she would probably be the first reporter on the property. The road from town took her past the Muldoon shaft, and while she couldn't see any smoke in the darkness, the stinging odor of burning timbers was thick in the air. By the time she reached the mine, she was gasping for breath. In her rush to get out the door, she had grabbed her best high-heeled dress shoes and her legs now ached from the mile-long walk.

The scene around the headframe was chaotic. One man was filling a skip with water from a hose. Other men were supplementing the work by running up with buckets of water, which they sloppily tossed into the skip before dashing back into the darkness. A few feet away from the collar of the shaft, Superintendent Garbarini and three other men worked on another skip with a cutting torch.

Pearl carefully made her way through the jumble of equipment, dodging a small group of excited miners who seemed to her to be doing little more than running in circles. The glare of the mine's helter-skelter array of bare lightbulbs accentuated the men's pale faces and cast long shadows that gave the scene a frightful air. She found a place away from the flurry and stood back, waiting to see a familiar face.

Because she grew up in Jackson, Pearl knew many of the miners and their families. She graduated from the local high school and was well known in the community for her journalistic endeavors. But on this night, at this place, she might as well have been a ghost or a piece of mining equipment. The mine employees were all focused on one thing—putting out the fire.

After a few minutes of watching the firefighting efforts, Pearl noticed Steve Pasalich filling kegs with water. She had met him only once before, while she was covering another story related to the mine, and it took her a minute to remember his name. When she walked up to him and said hello, he stared

Stockton Record Jackson bureau chief Pearl Wright.

back at her blankly—the feminine face and voice were no doubt strangely out of place. She apologized for interrupting his work.

Still dazed from the ordeal and standing solely because of the adrenaline pumping through his body, Pasalich welcomed the chance to stop for just a moment. Even more, he welcomed the opportunity to exorcise the terrifying memories of the past three hours. It didn't matter what Pearl's first question was—she was in the right place, with the right person, at the right time. Soon, she had the entire account of the discovery of the fire written down in shorthand. Minutes later, she was back at home, changing into more comfortable shoes as she called her editor and informed him of the breaking story. By the time she returned to the mine, the competition was already starting to arrive.

Immediately after he was contacted by Byron Pickard in the early morning hours of August 28, Hugh Wolfin of the Industrial Accident Commission informed the news wire services that a number of miners were trapped by a fire in the Argonaut Mine. Within minutes, every newspaper in the United States that owned a ticker-tape machine was aware of the situation and reporters were being rattled from their beds by ringing telephones. By sunrise, the Argonaut property was overrun with newspeople.

Swarming around the Argonaut shaft, reporters stopped rescue workers in midstride and demanded interviews. Anyone who looked like an employee of the mine was pursued and hounded for information. But no one was talking. Garbarini had given orders that no information of any kind was to be disclosed to outsiders.

Pearl Wright, however, had already scored a beat and scooped the competition. While other newspapers published best-guess accounts of the number of trapped miners, the *Stockton Record* was the first to accurately report that forty-seven men were trapped in the Argonaut Mine. Pearl had ascertained this information during her interview with Pasalich, who told her that he had delivered forty-seven lunch buckets that night. Pearl's first byline on the Argonaut story was accompanied by a subheader that read, "*Record* Branch Office Manager Covers Catastrophe." She was one of eight newswomen who would cover the Argonaut fire. Previously in California, only the 1920 Democratic Convention in San Francisco had drawn more female reporters.

*   *   *

In most newspapers published before World War I, news of the day took a back seat to the dramatic fiction and cosmopolitan essays that almost always graced the front page. But by the 1920s, reporters had found that with a little dramatization—and creative embellishment—news stories could appeal to a wide range of readers. A tragic event such as the Argonaut Mine disaster provided fertile ground for this reporting style, as this opening paragraph from a *Sacramento Bee* story of August 29, 1922, typifies:

> Depending on the feeling, emotions swept tauntingly between hope and despair through long hours of yesterday as wives, children, relatives, neighbors, and friends kept a rendezvous with the grim specter of death near the mouth of the main shaft of the Argonaut Mine. It was a crowd waiting outside the jury room of fate; anxious for the verdict the tireless little army of rescue workers strove to drag from the murky depths below. Anxious for the verdict, yet afraid of what it might mean. Thoughts shifted from the men working at the head of the little shaft to that unknown battle of those below, and involuntary shudders cut off visualizations ere they become too vivid.

At the Argonaut Mine, the army of newspeople steadily grew. A film crew from Pathe Newsreels, outfitted with hand-cranked motion picture cameras, was prepared to document rescue efforts for the enlightenment of moviegoers across the nation. Reporters from Sacramento and San Francisco were already well entrenched, having arrived throughout the morning hours by plane, train, automobile, and motorcycle. Because a significant number of the trapped miners were of Italian descent, the Italian-language newspapers *L'Italia* and *La Voce del Popolo* also sent reporters.

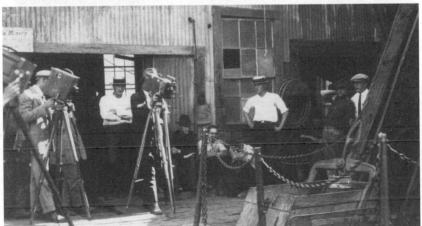

Cameramen for Pathe Newsreels train their cameras on the collar of the Argonaut shaft.

News photographers strolled about the property with their large, bellows-front Graflex cameras, capturing the blackened faces of firefighters and the poignant assemblage of waiting wives and children. At Jackson's tiny hilltop airport, pilots slept in their biplanes, ready to fly the latest photographs to Stockton, Sacramento, and San Francisco at a moment's notice. (The ability to send photographs by wire was still three years in the future.) Every available hotel room in Jackson was filled with newspeople and every available car had been rented.

By Monday afternoon, Superintendent Garbarini had had his fill of reporters interrupting the rescue effort and causing a general nuisance. Amador County sheriff, George Lucot, was called in to clear the property of anyone who was not either directly involved in the rescue efforts or a relative of one of the trapped men. Armed guards were then posted around the perimeter of the mine to assure that the reporters did not attempt to sneak back onto the property. When asked about the public's right to know, Garbarini retorted, "To hell with the public. This is the business of the company and the miners." In response, one of the first articles to be printed in the *Sacramento Bee* raged against the Argonaut chief's actions:

VEIL OF MYSTERY ADDS TO SORROW OF LOVED ONES

A veil of mystery thrown needlessly over the Argonaut Mine disaster adds to the anxiety and sorrow of relatives and friends of the entombed miners and left citizens of Jackson almost in the dark as to direct official information as to the progress of an event at their very doorsteps. . . . A censorship more stringent than that of the army in a time of war has stood like a Chinese wall between developments at the mine since Sunday night and the general public, through the policy of Superintendent V. S. Garbarini of refusing to let any information get out which is not already in general knowledge.

But reporters found no sympathy on the streets of Jackson. "We are all a big family here," a local man told an interviewer. "Mr. Garbarini has done a lot for our town."

Support for the Argonaut superintendent within the community was unwavering. If he said all that could be done was being done, then that was surely the case. But despite the outward appearance of enduring confidence, Garbarini was starting to question his own abilities. "If it was only a railroad wreck," he told his foreman, "I might be able to do something. It would be out in the open where I could see how to handle it and help the men. But this—it's all in the dark and beyond my reach."

Unable to obtain precise statements from knowledgeable sources, the press was left to speculate and assume, and the resulting news articles were filled with inaccuracies. Aware of the ongoing feud between the Argonaut and Kennedy mines, United Press reported that Hutchinson's offer to open the old connecting tunnel had been refused by Garbarini on Monday morning, when in fact the offer was not made until Monday evening and was accepted by Garbarini without hesitation.

One newspaper, frustrated by the inability to get direct information, printed the ramblings of a deranged old woman who professed to be a psychic. She claimed she had seen the entombed men in a dream, and that eight were dead and the others were dying.

Rumors quickly spread that no firefighting equipment had been maintained within the Argonaut Mine, as was called for by the Bureau of Mines safety standards; and that the Argonaut's supposed second exit, the Muldoon shaft, had been neglected, possibly to the point of becoming impassable. These allegations prompted an official statement from California's governor, William Stephens, that a thorough investigation would be held to determine if the charges were true.

In 1922, as today, nearly every U.S. city of any size had two or more strongly competitive newspapers, most of which were obviously biased toward the platform of a particular political party. If you lived in California's capital city, you read either the *Sacramento Bee;* its cross-town rival, the *Sacramento Union;* or the fledgling upstart *Sacramento Star.* The *Star*'s city editor, Ruth Finney, was a petite redhead who graduated from a San Jose normal school in 1918 and moved to Sacramento with her teacher's certificate in hand and absolutely no thought of becoming a cub reporter. But when her father's old friend, *Star* managing editor Bert Hews, offered her $15 a week—$5 more than she would have made as a teacher—she decided to give it a try.

"On my side of the balance sheet, I could list only red hair, a good grounding in grammar, a two-finger ability to type, an interest in politics and government, a habit of reading newspapers, and an acceptance of hard work as a matter of course," she later said. "The office was grubby, the ink-stained people in it often used profanity I had never heard before, and at any moment any of us might be hustled off to cover something in a part of the city I had never dreamed of going to. I vowed never to be a society editor or run a women's page, which shows how much I knew about small papers in small towns."

Still set on becoming a teacher, Ruth accepted the drudgery of reporting as a temporary inconvenience until she could be placed by the Sacramento County Board of Education. But when she wrote a story about the unfair wages teachers were receiving, she incurred the wrath of the county superintendent. When she went to renew her teaching certificate, she found that her records had been lost.

"My records were never found," she recalled. "I was never to become a teacher. My wagon was hitched to the *Star.*"

Ruth took a writing course at the University of California and read everything she could find on the subject of journalism. By 1922, she had survived four editors and two owners (Bert Hews was an early victim of the influenza epidemic), and had gained enough respect to be promoted to city editor, making, in her words, "the enormous sum of $25 a week" at age 24. She was the only person to ever hold that position at the *Star* and was at that time one of the highest paid female reporters at any newspaper in the Scripps-McRea (later Scripps-Howard) chain.

When Ruth learned the extent of the Argonaut tragedy, she recognized a rare opportunity to write hard copy. "A story broke in August 1922 that was made to order for me," she recalled. "I had to cover it myself, no matter what desk chores went undone at the *Sacramento Star*."

As daughter of John W. Finney, once California assemblyman and superintendent of the Telegraph Mine in Downieville, Ruth Finney had grown up in Gold Country and knew the language of mining—the meaning of stopes and drifts, and the dangers and difficulties of rescue operations. "This was no abstract tragedy to me," she remembered. "I felt so involved, so much a part of what was going on, that I couldn't bear to stand off and look at it from a distance."

While Ruth was not a flapper in the true sense of the term, she had quickly transformed herself from a prim and proper young girl into an archetypal modern businesswoman. Her comparatively generous salary allowed her to wear the latest fashions, including tailored business suits, colored leather pumps, Blue Moon silk stockings, and the obligatory contrasting cloche hat. Male reporters who mistook her femininity for weakness were quickly put in their place by her sharp tongue and Dorothy Parkeresque wit. Still, when she checked into her room at the National Hotel in Jackson on the morning of August 29, 1922, she felt apprehension over the quantity and quality of the competition.

"I've never competed with the cream of the crop before," she wrote in her diary. "The San Francisco papers have sent their best men. I'm all alone for our outfit."

Sacramento Star city editor Ruth Finney.

As Ruth Finney began the first of many long walks from her hotel to the Argonaut Mine, she could not have imagined how truly big this story would become or how much her life would be changed by the fateful days ahead.

8 A.M., Tuesday, August 29—Day 2

Tuesday was Election Day in Jackson. The race between California's incumbent governor, William Stephens, and his challenger for the Republican nomination, Friend Richardson, had been the hot topic in the little town's two competing newspapers during the past week. Now, talk at the polling places seldom strayed from the impending fate of the forty-seven trapped miners. Governor Stephens, who had just finished campaigning in Los Angeles, sent a telegram to the management of the Argonaut expressing his hope that the men would be found alive. A telegram was also received from entertainer Will Rogers, who had recently worked on a film in the Jackson area. Rogers also sent a check for $500 to aid the families of the miners.

Early Tuesday morning, representatives of the Bureau of Mines, the Industrial Accident Commission, and both the Argonaut and Kennedy mines again met with the idea of improving the efficiency of firefighting and rescue efforts through better organization. Nearly everyone agreed that a limited number of persons should have ultimate decision-making authority, and an executive committee of three was unanimously settled upon. V. S. Garbarini would chair the committee, Kennedy Mine president Hutchinson would serve as adviser, and IAC mining engineer Fred Lowell would act as secretary and press liaison.

In effect, members of the press had been invited to the Argonaut Mine by IAC superintendent Wolfin through his notification of the wire services on the first day of the fire. As soon as the executive committee was organized, Wolfin recommended that the press be allowed back on the property under more controlled conditions. The committee agreed to meet twice each day, and to issue regular bulletins that would keep the press and public informed of ongoing activities and the latest developments.

At the first meeting of the executive committee, the subject of reversing the Muldoon fan was brought up once again. The committee unanimously agreed that the flow of air should remain unchanged for the immediate future. It was still hoped that the trapped miners had situated themselves on the Kennedy side of the mine and that the suction of the Muldoon fan might be pulling fresh air in from the Kennedy workings.

The Industrial Accident Commission Executive
Committee: Kennedy Mine president E. C. Hutchinson,
Argonaut Mine superintendent V. S. Garbarini, and
secretary and press liaison Fred L. Lowell.

California State mineralogist Fletcher Hamilton, perhaps
the most respected mining man in the West, had been sent by
the governor to lend his expertise. He agreed with the decision
to keep the Muldoon fan running normally.

"The only thing to do was to keep the situation in status
quo," he later explained. "In other words, to keep it as it was in
the mine underground at that time, as the men had undoubtedly adapted themselves to the conditions prevailing; and if

they were in a dead end and able to bulkhead themselves in, they had done so under a certain condition, and if the condition had been changed, it might endanger the self-rescue they had attempted."

On the 3600 level of the Kennedy Mine, the rescue miners were encountering conditions even more challenging than expected. Because this level of the mine had been flooded to extinguish the encroaching Argonaut fire in 1919, much of the old drift was filled with great quantities of wet, sticky mud. Timbers had fallen across the drift in several areas, and these had to be carefully chopped out and hauled away. New supports were then put in place to assure the safety of the workers. At one point, the miners uncovered an old ore cart that took hours to extract from the gummy sludge.

Still ahead lay the first of two major obstacles: a planned bypass of a badly caved dogleg in the old drift. This shortcut would reduce the distance by one-third but required driving a crosscut in virgin ground, 60 feet through a solid greenstone wall. The miners expected to reach the location of the old dogleg and begin the crosscut in two days or less.

Additional rescue personnel arrived with Bureau of Mines Rescue Car #1 from Elko, Nevada. Newspapers reported that the Southern Pacific engine pulling this car broke all previous speed records for the route. Having been given priority right-of-way over all other trains on the line, the locomotive made the 139-mile trip in four hours, fifteen minutes.

With more than enough skilled men ready and able to do the work, neither Superintendent Garbarini nor Byron Pickard had given up the concept of rescuing the men through the Argonaut main shaft. There had always been logic in Garbarini's thought process. If the fire could be extinguished, it would definitely be quicker and easier to repair and reopen the burned portion of the shaft than to tunnel across from the Kennedy.

With the help of other knowledgeable mining engineers, Garbarini and Pickard developed a plan to smother the flames by creating an airtight bulkhead in the shaft above the fire. But first, the upper limits of the fire, now burning over several hundred feet of shaft, had to be extinguished.

A vacuum pipe was installed at the 2400 station so that firefighters could get a better look at the fire. Crews ran this pipe to the ventilation door on the Muldoon end of the 2400 drift, cut a hole in the door, inserted the pipe, then sealed everything to assure maximum draw. The suction of the Muldoon fan through this pipe was forceful enough to draw off the smoke from the area of the Argonaut shaft below the 2400 level. Firefighters could now clearly see that the upper limit of the fire was burning across the full width of the passageway, about 60 feet below the 2500 station.

A second pipe was then installed to bring an inexhaustible supply of water from the surface that could be applied directly to the fire. Special valves were put in place to increase the force of the water so that it could be shot from a safe distance. Two hundred feet of canvas fire hose was connected to the end of the water pipe and carried down the manway ladder to within 10 feet of the fire by a team of apparatus men. Five additional men were stationed above the firefighters to relay messages to the 2400 station, where another crewman was waiting to relay orders to the surface by telephone. With everything in place, the water valve was opened to full capacity.

For the first time, water was being directed exactly where it was needed and the resulting steam that had imperiled previous firefighting crews was now being drawn away by the vacuum pipe. It took only minutes for the firefighters to extinguish the upper limit of the fire. Crews were then assigned to watch the area throughout the night to assure that the fire was permanently out. The following morning, a team of carpenters would build a bulkhead to seal off the shaft and hopefully smother the lower limits of the fire.

4 P.M., Monday, August 29—Day 2

Eight hundred feet below, beyond the blackened expanse of shaft that was visible to firefighters, the lower limit of the fire still raged. The amount of fuel that was being consumed by the flames could be estimated by watching the quantity of smoke emanating from the Muldoon fan. The Bureau of Mines called in their chief consulting chemical engineer, Dr. Lionel H. Duschak, to take regular samples of these emissions for analysis.

A former chemist for Corning Glass Works in New York, Dr. Duschak had been employed by the bureau either directly or indirectly since 1913, primarily in conducting various studies at the bureau's Pacific Experiment Station at the University of California at Berkeley. Mining engineers who wanted to be brought up to date on the latest techniques in metallurgical and chemical analysis needed only to attend one of Duschak's lectures at the university.

Among the arsenal of high-tech equipment that Duschak brought to the Argonaut was a newly developed color-coded carbon monoxide detector, which was used there for the first time in any mine. By carefully bratticing the Muldoon fan, Duschak was able to get undiluted samples of the air being pulled from the Argonaut's lower levels. Despite the upper limits of the fire having been extinguished, his analysis showed that the air being exhausted by the ventilation system was filled with deadly carbon monoxide gas. It was his opinion that the lower limit of the fire was still aggressively consuming wooden timbers.

*　　*　　*

On Tuesday evening, a telegram from the president of Argonaut Mining and Milling Company was delivered to Superintendent Garbarini's office:

New York City, N.Y.
August 29, 1922
V. S. Garbarini, General Manager
Argonaut Mine, Jackson, Calif.

Hoping that this last disaster will not involve lives of the men that are now in such great jeopardy. Spare no expense or money to save your men and mitigate the disaster their families face, the welfare of the mine being the last and least consideration.

John T. Smith 5:45 P.M.

Smith also wired $1000 to be used for the aid and comfort of the wives and children of the trapped miners.

Later that night, after considerable urging and with a promise that he would personally remain on the property throughout the night to keep an eye on things, Fletcher Hamilton convinced Superintendent Garbarini to go home and get some sleep. The Argonaut manager had not even taken a nap since Sunday night. Reluctantly, Garbarini dragged himself into his car and drove home. He would be back before sunrise.

Ruth Finney's first few days in Jackson were filled with both excitement and drudgery, as she later described in her unpublished autobiography:

I took a room at the National Hotel, at one end of Main Street, and began a routine of day and night trips to the two mines for bulletins to catch deadlines of the western and eastern morning and afternoon papers served by United Press.

Between bulletins I wrote detailed accounts of rescue operations, the atmosphere in the town, and the views of federal and state mine officials about probable causes of the disaster and whether ventilating fans at the Argonaut should or should not have been reversed. There were stories to be done about the families of the buried men, and how they were enduring the fear and suspense.

Some of the reporters who were covering the disaster brought portable typewriters, and occasionally someone would loan one to Ruth for an hour or two. But, for the most part, her stories were written in longhand, then taken to the Western Union office in downtown Jackson for transmittal by telegraph to *Sacramento Star* editor Harold Matson. Calling in news copy by telephone was a luxury reserved for important breaks in the story and required waiting to be connected to Jackson's elusive outside line. The town was served by a single trunk line that carried both incoming and outgoing calls between Jackson and other cities. During busy periods, a caller might have to wait several hours to have a long distance call put through.

As a representative of both the *Sacramento Star* and United Press wire service, Ruth worked out a friendly arrangement with Tom Trebell of Associated Press to share the night watch, permitting each of them a few hours of sleep between shifts. Even then, she would sleep in her clothes so that she would be ready for action at a moment's notice. Finney and Trebell also shared the duty of running copy to the Western Union office, agreeing to alternate whose story was sent first.

Even in the "modern" 1920s, female reporters were typically sent to cover only the more emotional elements of a story. Ruth's first article on the Argonaut fire, published in the *Star* under the headline "If It's Like This Above—What's It Like Below?" is typical of work produced by a "sob sister"—the contemporaneous term for female reporters who specialized in a sentimental and highly maudlin style of writing:

Jackson, Aug. 29—They are forming on the hillside, silent, waiting.

Hundreds of eyes fixed on the mouth of the shaft, never wavering. Strong men, helpless, standing there. Nothing they can do.

Women, dry eyed, silent.

Children—hushed, quiet, some of them asleep on the rockpiles or lumber.

Through the night a dozen electric lights, the ghostly outlines of the hoist, piles of lumber and silent people, standing and waiting.

And then when dawn came, grey and pallid across the valley, the white stones of a little cemetery.

Still huddled in groups, numb with terror, too stunned to feel.

And every minute through the night, the gasps grow denser, more choking, gas and smoke, suffocating the workers and the people who wait.

"And if it is like this up here—what's below?—"

"There's hope—you've got to hope."

Then the cry of the skip bell, and even more intense silence. Workers coming up after their shift and others going down.

Horrible through the night, blackness, the choking, but when morning came—

The sun, warmth, air, a little valley, blue and purple hills around it—beautiful, peaceful.

And down beneath—4800 feet down—blackness, death, fire—the horrible tomb of 43 men. Men and women in the sunlight, tortured because they are alive and well and can do nothing for the men below.

It may be weeks before men can get to the bodies. The fire is growing worse.

They cannot smother it for fear of smothering the men if they should chance to be alive. They cannot flood it for fear of drowning the men. Workers cannot get to the flames because of the smoke.

They are going down ten at a time, staying as long as they can, lowering water, a skip full at a time, to fight the flames.

By comparison, Ruth's contemporary from the *Stockton Record*, Pearl Wright, wrote in a journalistic style that was dramatic, yet straightforward, realistic, and all business:

Jackson Office *Stockton Record*, Aug. 29—Volumes of nauseating gas issuing from the burning depths of the Argonaut mine at Jackson through the Muldoon air shaft lead to the belief that the forty-seven men who were imprisoned in the bowels of the earth at midnight Sunday by a fire which cut off their escape have all perished.

Notwithstanding the seeming hopelessness of the task, however, the mine rescue crews are sticking desperately to their task and every possible effort is being bent toward reaching the entombed men.

Ruth Finney and Pearl Wright started out on two very different paths. While Ruth was attending normal school and preparing for her career as a teacher, Pearl was learning the craft of writing and reporting. But fate would eventually put them on the same course. Both were hired by major California newspapers at a young age. Both quickly moved into positions of responsibility—Ruth as the *Sacramento Star* city editor and Pearl as the *Stockton Record* bureau manager in Amador County.

Both were prime examples of the *new woman* of the 1920s. Women who had finally been given the right to vote in 1919; who had shed coifed tresses and long skirts for bobbed hair and more than a glimpse of stocking; who had already proven they could handle a man's job and thrive in a man's world.

Much of what would be written about the Argonaut disaster would come from the pens of these two women. But what they wrote and how they wrote it would take them in two surprisingly different directions.

CHAPTER 6

In Her Dark, Frightened Eyes

The number of miners who made their way to Jackson in the days immediately following the discovery of the fire was overwhelming. They came from the hundreds of mines that dotted California's Mother Lode, as well as from Nevada and Arizona. They arrived at the Argonaut Mine hoping to help in whatever way possible with the rescue of their trapped comrades. When asked why so many miners would come so far without being asked, one of them answered, "You see, it might be our turn next."

Although only a small percentage of this reserve of volunteer miners was used in the firefighting and rescue efforts, neither the Bureau of Mines nor Argonaut Mine management had the heart to turn them away. They wandered about the mine property, watching for opportunities to lend a hand and augmenting the ever-present throng of onlookers.

The dramatic scene unfolding around the Argonaut headframe was described by Tom Trebell of the Associated Press in one of the first articles he wrote after arriving at the mine:

Around a far-flung roped-off circle in which the weather beaten upper works of the Argonaut main shaft is the hub, are the relatives of the trapped men, knots of the merely curious and the morbid. The tear bedewed faces of the children are everywhere to be seen, while silent women aproned and hatless, wait upon every sound and every word, and try to translate from them some inkling of hope. Some of them are standing in the cool night air, just as they left their cook stoves and their gardens hours before determined to keep up the vigil until the end.

"Assigned as the guardian over these women is an entirely different class of feminine temperament," reported the *San Francisco Call*, "the Red Cross workers, recruited from among the wives of the businessmen of Jackson. Psychologists would find a startling contrast between these two types of women. Five days ago, they would meet on the street as strangers. Today these two, welded by a common compassion, are hoping side by side."

Like many other residents of Jackson, the Red Cross Amador County chapter president, Mary Warrington, had been awakened from a comfortable sleep on Monday morning by the town's dedicated switchboard operator. But this time, the request for assistance came directly from V. S. Garbarini. Warrington never anticipated being involved in a disaster of this magnitude, but many years of training had prepared her to do whatever was necessary to provide aid and comfort.

By sunrise on Monday morning, Warrington and a small company of Red Cross nurses had commandeered a building on the Argonaut property and established a full-service canteen and first aid station. The organization's first concern was the families of the entombed men, who were arriving at the mine in increasing numbers. The nurses equipped their station with cots

Gathering of workers and waiting volunteers at the collar of the Argonaut shaft.

and chairs for the miners' families, they established food service for both the families and rescue workers, and they ordered in a full stock of medical supplies, as well as beds, mattresses, and bedclothes. During the first sixty hours of the Argonaut fire, Warrington did not leave her station except to take a short nap.

Meals and coffee were provided to family and volunteers around the clock. An open box attached to the wall just outside the canteen door was kept full of cigarettes. Beds were available for the sick and injured, or for those who just needed a rest. But the toughest challenge was providing moral support for both the families of the entombed men and the tireless army of rescue workers. Warrington admonished her ladies to keep a positive attitude. "Smiles," she told her crew. "Smiles and positivity, no matter what rumors you hear or what pessimisms you may harbor."

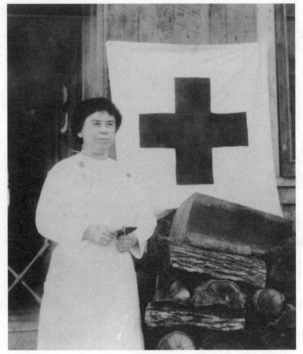

Mary Warrington, president, Amador County chapter
of the American Red Cross.

The ladies were particularly watchful of the pregnant wives
of trapped miners Elia Pavlovich and George Steinman. There
were also a number of other women who just seemed to be taking the ordeal particularly hard. Some of them did not speak
sufficient English to let their needs be known. Others simply
kept to themselves, refusing even food and water until it was
forced upon them.

A reporter for the *Sacramento Bee* described the plight of
waiting wives and family:

> From early yesterday morning, these women have been
> waiting. Their nerves unstrung, fighting back the tears.

As many as possible have been induced to return to their homes, but many refuse, especially those whose homes are not in Jackson. Some have come from Sutter Creek and Amador City, and will not leave until definite word comes from below. These, the Red Cross women try to cheer up with bits of conversation. The wives and relatives of the entombed men listen without hearing. Their fingers twisting handkerchiefs aimlessly, their eyes staring forward blankly. A huge pile of blue shale across the road stares back, raising layers of palpitating heat, reflecting from its sides the despair that surges through these women's souls.

On the first morning of the ordeal, Warrington noticed the wife of trapped miner Mike Vujovich standing very near the Argonaut shaft. Warrington approached her slowly from behind and quietly asked if she needed help. "If I know my man is dead," the woman said without turning, "I throw myself down there." Warrington put her arm around the woman and guided her back toward the first aid station. From that moment on, the Red Cross staff was charged with keeping a watchful eye on the Argonaut shaft. Any family member who wandered too close was quickly led in another direction.

Linda Steinman, while pregnant, was among the most stoic of the wives. Standing in the shade of the Red Cross shelter, with dark shadows under her eyes and lines of anxiety across her forehead, she told reporters,

> If my husband comes out of the mine, I know it will be a miracle granted by God. If he does not come back to me, I shall know that it was not meant by Him that he should return. . . . I must wearily drag my way through life no matter how heavy the burden may be. I hope for the best, and if it don't come, well, I have four children to live for. They are all boys, and such a comfort. But,

Members of the American Red Cross at the Argonaut Mine with chapter president Mary Warrington at center.

by the God who rules above, they shall never descend into a mine as long as I live.

8 A.M., Wednesday, August 30—Day 3

As of Wednesday morning, the Argonaut miners had been trapped for two and a half days, and crews working to clear the Kennedy 3600 drift had made little progress. After a lengthy meeting with mining engineer W. E. Downs, the executive committee decided to start a second rescue effort, on the Kennedy 3900 level. Like the 3600, the Kennedy 3900 drift had been sealed after the 1919 fire and allowed to deteriorate. Over 300 feet of the old drift had collapsed and would need to be excavated and retimbered. Once the caved ground was cleared, 140 feet of solid rock lay between the end of the Kennedy 3900 and the rescuers' final goal—a crosscut extending out of the Argonaut 4600 station.

Cigars & Cigarettes for mine rescue workers and relatives of miners

ONLY.

Meals for Mine rescue workers, relatives of miners and Red Cross workers.

At the entrance to the Red Cross canteen, an unknown volunteer poses with a caged canary that will be used by rescue workers to detect carbon monoxide gas.

Later that morning, the management of the Argonaut Mine finally confirmed what reporter Pearl Wright had reported the first day of the fire—that forty-seven miners were missing. This official count was based on a brass check identification system, some form of which was used at most large mines. At the beginning of every shift, after each man changed into his work clothes and completed the inspection process, he picked up a brass check from a pegboard hanging near the exit of the change house. This little metal disk, sort of a miner's dog tag, was stamped with a number that was also written next to the miner's name on the shift roster. At the end of his shift, he placed the check back on the board, indicating that he was back above ground and finished for the day.

Fifty-two brass checks were missing from the board at the Argonaut. Five of these belonged to men who returned to the surface: shift boss Clarence Bradshaw; skip tender Steve Pasalich; tender's helper Mitchell Jogo; and two miners who had been working above the 3000-foot level. Once the remaining checks were inventoried, an official list of the trapped miners' names was released to the press.

By the third day of the fire, the mood in Jackson began to shift from anxious optimism to disappointment and frustration. Even with fifty apparatus men and a trained army of firefighters working around the clock, the Argonaut shaft was still on fire, and the excavation of the Kennedy 3600 had barely begun. It seemed to most people that the tunneling effort at the Kennedy had been started too late, and now its completion was expected to take far longer than originally planned. The town was filled with mining experts and rescue crews, yet no real progress had been made toward freeing the trapped miners.

Everyone in Jackson had an opinion about the decision not to shut down the Muldoon fan. The subject was debated at cafe tables, across store counters, and on sidewalk benches. Even those who remained among Superintendent Garbarini's staunchest supporters wondered how he could be right when the answer seemed so logical—the fan was pulling the smoke and gas down to the levels where the men were working. Why not shut it off?

While daily commerce went on as usual, the mood of the townspeople reflected their preoccupation with the tragic event that was unfolding so near their hearts and homes but over which they had no control. Had it not been for the Argonaut fire, many of the town's residents would have been working on Amador County's display for the state fair—a yearly opportunity for counties to tout their contribution to the California economy and enter into friendly competition with neighboring counties. As soon as the Amador County Chamber of Commerce heard about the trapped miners, they withdrew the county's entry. "Pending the verdict of fate holding this county in paralysis," said the formal press release, "we cannot enter into the work in the proper spirit."

The spot reserved for Amador County's display did not remain empty, however. When the fair opened, visitors found a large photograph of the Argonaut Mine draped in purple and black, accompanied by a vase of purple and white flowers and a printed panel that read

> Amador County, due to the Argonaut tragedy, withdrew its exhibit. The 36 counties of California exhibiting in this building completed the booth, and do this as a tribute to their sister county of Amador, now in sorrow.

Born of the California Gold Rush and nurtured into the twentieth century by its productive deep-rock gold mines, the town of Jackson in 1922 was the bustling county seat for one of California's most productive gold mining counties. The towering headframes of both the Argonaut and Kennedy mines were clearly visible from Jackson's main street, and their thundering stamp mills, as well as those of a half-dozen other mines, rattled both the downtown businesses and the various ethnic neighborhoods that skirted the town. Because the richest part of the Mother Lode ran through Amador County, the nearby towns of Sutter Creek, Amador City, and Plymouth boasted rich mines as well, making the area a magnet for job-seeking immigrants.

Just weeks after gold was discovered on the American River in 1848, miners were panning the gravels of Jackson Creek, 25 miles to the south, where they found handfuls of smooth yellow nuggets called placer gold. In addition to Americans who came from the East Coast by land and sea, the rush of California immigration that came after the discovery of gold brought a melting pot of miners, gamblers, and merchants from countries around the globe, including France, Mexico, Chile, and China, among others. Soon, the banks of Jackson Creek were crowded with red-shirted, scruffy-bearded men living in tattered tents and struggling to pull $15 in gold each day from the icy, mountain-fed stream.

In the winter of 1849, Frenchman Louis Tellier built a make-shift structure near the confluence of the three branches of Jackson Creek and opened a general store. Soon, some of the less successful miners realized that returning to their former professions would pay just as well as panning the cold waters of the streams and would require far less manual labor. Within a season, the camp had a hotel and a host of saloons—then blacksmiths, lawyers, and doctors.

It didn't take long for the placer miners to recognize that the gold in Amador County's streams came from somewhere higher up, and a year had barely passed before the surrounding hillsides were dotted with excavations. These were the forerunners of the rich deep-rock gold mines of the twentieth century.

From a single tent store, Jackson grew into a rip-roaring gold rush boomtown with strong French and Chinese influences. Over the decades, the town bounced back from several devastating fires and floods, then faded a bit in the late nineteenth century when the rush dwindled and gold mining became a bona fide industry.

With the new century came new technology that allowed mines to drive their shafts deeper and extract gold more quickly. These new mines needed a workforce, and waves of immigrants once again rushed to Amador County. The French and Chinese population, which had gradually dispersed, was quickly supplanted by a melting pot of refugees from war-torn Southern Europe and the Balkan states. By the end of World War I, Jackson had settled into its old ways. The Roaring Twenties would secure its reputation as a wide-open mining town.

A view of Main Street, Jackson, California, as seen from the National Hotel. The Argonaut Mine is just visible on the distant hill.

Although California voters helped ratify the Eighteenth Amendment, establishing Prohibition, the state was not, nor would it ever be, a dry state. Both the amendment and the associated Volstead Act of 1919 were full of loopholes that allowed anyone with any degree of ambition to obtain alcoholic beverages. In California's cities, bootleggers produced large quantities of whiskey, rum, and gin. In rural areas such as Jackson, clandestine wineries and backyard stills provided more than enough hooch to satisfy the needs of the miners and others inclined to imbibitions. Many of Jackson's saloon owners had been clever enough to put in a stock of top-quality legal booze prior to Prohibition's effective date. This well-hidden and carefully rationed treasure only added to the town's iniquitous appeal.

After work, the miners of Amador County had a variety of amusements from which to choose. While most of the married men went directly to their waiting families, those who were single or living alone often took the long way home. Like the mines, the speakeasies, gambling halls, and brothels of Jackson never closed.

On Main Street, with the advent of Prohibition, saloon signs were replaced by soft drink parlor signs. Inside the front door of these seemingly benign establishments there was every indication that they were exactly what was advertised. Women and children came and went throughout the day, enjoying sparkling glasses of root beer, seltzers, and phosphates. Only the most observant person might notice that the parlor seemed to take up less than a quarter of the depth of the building. Beyond the facade was a saloon or speakeasy, discreetly accessed through a well-guarded side or back door. Sporadic raids by federal officers were seldom more than an inconvenience, occasionally prompting the proprietor to move his or her establishment to a new location.

For decades, Jackson's saloons had been the domain of the male, but the new woman of the 1920s would not be shut out of any activity, or any establishment. While it is highly unlikely that a female who frequented the speakeasies would have been considered a "nice girl" my members of the predominantly conservative community-at-large, these women, and the men who drank alongside them, saw nothing iniquitous about their participation in that very communal atmosphere. There was, however, another element of the fairer sex who "knew their place" in the community and whose self-imposed isolation was essential to their survival.

Along Jackson Creek, which divided downtown Jackson from the southerly boardinghouse district, a number of small shacks housed the miners' other vice. Discreetly referred to as ladies' dormitories, the services they provided were certainly no more lawful than booze or gambling but required less camouflage because of their quiet nature. The women who worked

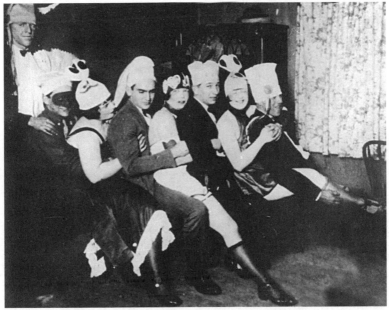

Some frolicking Jackson residents pose for a classic "flapper" party picture.

there were as ethnically diverse as their clientele, and the willing companionship of a female from the "home country" was as alluring to the foreign miner as the other services being purveyed. The ladies charged for their time, and how the men used it was up to them. Where 49ers once mined the stream of gold, fallen women now mined the miners for their weekly paycheck.

Regardless of their popularity and tolerability, gambling, booze, and prostitution were illegal, and local law officials could not entirely look the other way. Under the occasional scrutiny of federal authorities, Amador County sheriff George Lucott arrested enough local moonshiners and madams to give the appearance of compliance with both state and federal laws—although how or why he chose those specific unfortunate individuals from the sea of prospective offenders is open to speculation.

Even after the mines were closed at the beginning of World War II, gambling and prostitution remained among Jackson's busiest commercial enterprises. The town's last brothel was closed in 1956, when California's newly reelected attorney general, Edmund "Pat" Brown, made good on a campaign promise to eliminate prostitution in the state.

For the hundreds of mine workers who populated the area, these establishments provided a badly needed escape from their perilous workday world. After eight to ten backbreaking hours in a dark, damp hole in the ground, a miner could find remedy anytime of the day or night in a glass of cheap gin, the bright lights and noisy activity of a gambling hall, or the gentle ministrations of a professional female.

Like many small towns, Jackson had always been wary of both newcomers and visitors who overstayed their welcome. For the moment, mining experts, volunteer miners, and state officials had a reason to be there. Members of the press—especially the "big city" press—were seen as interlopers. Ruth Finney recalled:

> It was inevitable that the town resented us. By the second week in September, the crowd of reporters had swelled to about a hundred. We had virtually taken over the hotel, were demanding food at all hours, and were filling the place with the sound of clacking typewriters. The newspapermen were crowding into saloons and all the places that served food, overrunning the small telephone company office and demanding that more trunk lines be installed, forcing the store where the Western Union wire was installed to keep open at unheard of hours.

Wherever the reporters gathered, there would inevitably be lighthearted conversation and laughter that was offensive to the townspeople. Many were angered by newspeople who constantly hounded grief-stricken family members for interviews. Others simply didn't like what was being written. On one occasion, a group of men seized a bundle of San Francisco newspapers and tore them up before they could be distributed.

Ruth tried her best to be inconspicuous but found it nearly impossible under the circumstances:

> The town was so small that whenever we stepped out of the hotel we were in the center of things. And we had to step out constantly, for there were no telephones in our rooms and no phones anywhere that connected with the mines. We were forced to run the gauntlet of hostile townspeople whether we walked to the Argonaut offices at the other end of the main street, or rented a car to drive to the vicinity of the Kennedy Mine.

The *San Francisco Examiner* reported that Jackson was a "town peopled by foreigners." Since that newspaper's broad definition of "foreign" included even long-term naturalized citizens, the statement was very true. The greater percentage of Jackson's 2500 residents had been born in a foreign country. The forty-seven men trapped in the Argonaut Mine were representative of the area's ethnic population: Seventeen were born in Italy; eleven in Balkan states, including Dalmatia, Herzegovina, Montenegro, Serbia, and Yugoslavia; two were Spaniards; two were from Sardinia; two from Austria; and one each from Germany, Portugal, Sweden, and Switzerland. Nine of the men had been born in the United States.

In 1917 and 1921, the U.S. Congress had enacted controversial immigration laws that greatly limited the number of foreigners allowed to enter the United States, especially from Southern Europe. These laws were nationally popular because the war had instilled a sense of nativism among many Americans with old roots in Northern and Central Europe. Such laws were not popular with mine owners, however, since immigrants from Southern Europe made up a great percentage of the mining workforce. Relatively few native-born Americans had significant underground mining experience and even fewer were willing to perform dangerous and backbreaking labor for the average mining wage of $4 a day.

"Psychologists would find this a rich realm," wrote Herb Westen of the *San Francisco Call*. "Any outward emotion that is being made evident is mostly by the Anglo Saxon women and not by the Serbian and Italian wives of those who are 'somewhere below.'"

Serbians and others of Balkan origin made up a notable portion of the Jackson community in 1922 and still do today. A significant number of Serbian families settled in the area during the California Gold Rush, and by 1922, this well-established ethnic community with the oldest Serbian church in the western United States was attracting even more Serbian immigrants. Jackson's mining community was especially inviting to those men who had been miners in the mineral-rich Carpathian Mountains of their homeland.

Argonaut miner Niko Stanicich brought his new wife, Mary, to America from Serbia in 1913. The Balkan Wars—a precursor to World War I—had left the region politically and financially unstable, and the young couple hoped for a prosperous new life in America. They settled in Montana, where Niko quickly found work in the booming copper mines. In the happy years that followed, Mary gave him two sons and a daughter.

In 1920, Niko heard about the gold mines of Jackson and the area's extensive Serbian community and church. He decided to visit the town to check out the potential for work. He never returned to Montana. Within a few days of his arrival, he took a job at the Kennedy Mine and sent for his wife and children.

In April 1922, Niko left the Kennedy Mine for a better-paying job at the Argonaut.

While the Serbian community was centered in the church, the cultural cornerstone of the Italian community was the Italian Benevolent Society, organized in Jackson in 1881. By 1922, most of the area's Italians were second-generation and old-line first-generation families who came to California in the mid-nineteenth century. Accordingly, Italian miners at the Argonaut and Kennedy mines were a combination of California-born Italian-Americans and newly arrived immigrants, who, like the Serbs, were attracted to Jackson's well-established ethnic community and the availability of work in the mines.

Italian miner Giuseppe Giorza and his wife, Virginia, lived with their five children in a small cottage on Kennedy Flat, not far from the mines. To supplement Giuseppe's meager $3.75 a day salary, the Giorzas kept a milk cow and tended a small truck garden, selling milk and fresh vegetables to the Italian neighborhood. Like Niko Stanicich, Giuseppe Giorza made the ill-fated decision to move from the Kennedy to the Argonaut Mine.

After the third day of the fire, when it became clear that the rescue effort was going to be protracted, Virginia Giorza stayed at the cottage and busied herself with tending the garden and the children. Red Cross volunteers and members of the Italian Benevolent Society dropped by throughout the day to bring her the latest news and deliver donations of food and clothing.

"The mother knows of the plight of the family," Pearl Wright reported, "yet to her children, she admits nothing. Outwardly she is calmly reserved, though inwardly she is fighting a great battle."

Pearl watched as fourteen-year-old Louis Giorza made daily visits to the mine. "The boy has almost refused to eat since the news came to the top during the early hours of last Monday morning that his father and forty-six other men were at the bottom of the mine, cut off from escape by flames. . . . He sits for hours every day, watching the mouth of the shaft. . . . Each time the top of an ascending skip appears he leaps to his feet and looks anxiously. Then with fallen face he drops back upon the plank. Thus far, daddy has not been a passenger."

One afternoon, Pearl noticed a new face among the familiar throng of miners' relatives standing in the shade of the Red Cross station. He was an elderly gentleman, very obviously American, wearing plain clothes and a weathered hat. She approached and asked him which of the miners he was related to. He told her he was the father of miner Bert Seamans and that he had been searching for his son for many years. When he saw the list of the entombed Argonaut miners in the newspaper, he quickly made his way to Jackson and confirmed that it was in fact his long-lost son who was among the men trapped in the mine.

Reporters uncovered more than a few revelations about the miners and the assembled crowd of waiting friends and relatives. They learned that trapped miner Elmer Bacheller was not a regular employee of the mine but had taken the place of a friend who wanted to go on vacation. They discovered that Luigi Oliva, now working on the rescue crew, was scheduled for the Sunday night shift but took the day off to visit friends in San Francisco. His brother, Pio, was among those trapped in the mine.

Several of the Argonaut miners had recently returned from military service. Rade Lajovich, a native of Montenegro, served in the U.S. Army throughout World War I. Peter Bagoye was a six-year veteran of the Austrian Army. Just four months earlier, he left his family to come to California and join his friend Paul Delonga at the Argonaut. Bagoye had recently written a letter to his wife, telling her that he was now settled in Jackson and ready for her to join him.

Earlier in the year, many of the miners had appeared as extras in the silent movie *The Beloved Unknown,* which was filmed on the Argonaut property and other Jackson area locations. The film's star, Holbart Bosworth, sent a representative of his production company to Jackson to offer whatever aid they might provide to the families of the trapped men.

Miner Battista Manachino, once an expert baker in Italy, had recently accepted a position with a local bakery in Jackson. He had given notice to the Argonaut management that Sunday would be his last day at the mine.

Myrtle Richards, fiancée of James Clayton, came to the mine day after day, hoping against hope that fate would not deal her a second devastating blow. Just one year earlier, Myrtle's first husband was killed in a mining accident. James Clayton stopped by her house on his way to the mine that fateful Sunday evening to see how work was proceeding on her trousseau.

Clayton's two brothers worked on the rescue crew, and one of them, Valentine Clayton, was extremely critical of the slow progress of the rescue effort. He recommended the use of a conveyor belt to more quickly move rock and debris out of the rescue drifts. He presented his theory to the executive committee, and when his plan was rejected by Garbarini, Valentine became highly agitated and insisted on giving a demonstration. Fred Lowell told him he would arrange an appointment with the committee the following day, but when Clayton showed up at the mine offices, the sheriff was waiting to escort him from the property.

Trapped in the mine with James Clayton was his best friend, Charles Fitzgerald. Charles had been separated from his wife for nearly two years, but when Frances Fitzgerald learned that her husband was among the entombed miners, she returned to Jackson to keep vigil with the other wives.

When the Fitzgeralds parted ways, Frances took her daughter, Janet, with her to live in Oakland, leaving their young son

Members of the ill-fated Argonaut late shift are among the actors in this still shot taken on the Jackson set of the film *The Beloved Unknown.*

behind with Charles. When she arrived at the mine, she found seven-year-old Donald waiting patiently for his father to come up from a seemingly endless shift. An attractive young woman was keeping watch over the boy, and Frances was about to thank her for her kindness when one of the Red Cross nurses called out for Mrs. Fitzgerald, and both women answered.

According to newspaper accounts, Emily Ludekins had been living with Charles Fitzgerald long enough to be accepted by the mining community as his wife. Frances Fitzgerald was not shy in interviews with reporters. "I don't know that I will go back to him if he is alive," she told the *San Francisco Examiner.* "When I have done all I can for him, I may go back to Oakland. But I am his wife. While he is in danger I am here to stand by him and help when I can. And he—well, he is the father of my little boy and girl. And that's what counts."

The plight of waiting wives was ample fodder for female reporters relegated to writing sob-sister stories such as this tearjerker from reporter Mila Landis of the *Sacramento Bee:*

Argonaut miner
James Clayton in
his World War I
uniform.

Flashes of light are set back from twinkling dinner pails
as the men of the day shift trudge home in lines radi-
ating in all directions from the Kennedy Mine. From
the front porches of the cottages on the steep Jackson
hillsides, the wives of the imprisoned miners watch
these tell-tale flashes of light. [T]hey have not prepared
lunches for the men. [N]o miner's lunch pail has clashed
against the sagging gate as a father stoops down to pick
up the children who run to meet him.

Tragic figure among the waiting dozen wives is Mrs.
M. Stanicich. Like a wild frightened thing, this little

foreign woman backs away from the door of her home
when visitors, kindly of purpose, approach her. For all
she can tell, their words of sympathy may be threats of
eviction or news that the rescue work, after all, has
been entirely in vain, for the foreign tongue is a mystery
to her. In her dark, frightened eyes, there is despair, terror, and sorrow.

Like other small towns in Northern California's Sierra Foothills, Jackson was far removed from the country's mainstream.
Radio was still in its infancy. The community's several newspapers provided no national or world news coverage. Only occasional editorials on national politics and human interest stories
hinted at national trends. Jackson's primary connections with
the outside world were the big city newspapers and the Ratto
Theater.

A classic small-town theater with art deco styling, the Ratto
had changed with the times, quickly graduating from minstrel
shows, chautauquas, and band concerts, to silent films and newsreels (supplemented by the occasional boxing match). On Sunday, August 27, 1922, the day the fire was discovered in the
Argonaut, the Ratto premiered *The Fox*, a silent western starring
Harry Carry, Sr., with accompanying music from a live orches-
tra. News stories highlighted in the Pathe newsreel included the
rise of Mussolini and the Fascist party in Italy, Johnny Weiss-
muller's record-breaking 100-meter swim, the American railroad strike, and the death of Alexander Graham Bell.

Few in Jackson knew or cared that the Pathe newsreel failed
to mention that Pope Pius X was urging a campaign against the
current trend of "revealing" women's fashions, or that James
Joyce's *Ulysses* had been banned in the United States, or that
groundbreaking treatments for diabetes and tuberculosis had just
been perfected. The community and the mines had developed a

In a photograph that predates the disaster, an unidentified group of Argonaut miners prepares to enter the mine through the main shaft.

perfect symbiosis that cultivated independence from, and apathy toward, the outside world. The events unfolding at the Argonaut Mine would test their indifference.

Herb Weston, a popular columnist of the period, philosophized:

> Students of human nature would find this 1922 world, as visualized by Jackson, an esoteric sort of thing. Picture the town—stoical, matter of fact, without temperament—daring God and Nature as in the days of '49. There is no general hysteria here. Miners congregate on the street corners and calmly discuss the catastrophe—a thing alphabetically categorized in the scheme of things daring. . . . The women folk sit around prepared for widowhood while the men, except the entombed forty-seven, hurl water, 5000 gallons at a time, down into the depths of this inferno. Relieved, the men proceed to town to get refreshments, then to their beds for a brief surcease from the heartbreaking toil.

4 P.M., Wednesday, August 30—Day 3

Late Wednesday afternoon, all work was called to a halt as mine management, family members, and volunteers gathered at the Argonaut shaft to pray for the safe delivery of the trapped miners. Representatives of the Methodist, Greek Orthodox, and Catholic churches expressed in brief statements what the assembled throng felt in their hearts. As the ceremony came to a close, the volunteers returned to work, and many of the wives and family members who had been at the mine for almost four days began to make their way homeward. Among those remaining on the property was the wife of Ernie Miller. As she said goodbye to the departing wives, one of them put her arms around Catherine Miller and pulled her close. "Your husband very smart," she said. "Maybe he get my man out."

CHAPTER 7

Disappointments and Conflicts

4 P.M., Tuesday, September 5—Day 9

At the Kennedy 3600 station, Bill Sinclair pushed down the detonator plunger and waited for the familiar rumble. It only took a few seconds for the sound to reach the rescue crew—a quick succession of booms followed by a soft vibration in the station floor a few seconds later. A strategically placed series of dynamite charges had just demolished the last remaining bit of greenstone in a crosscut designed to bypass the old dogleg in the Kennedy 3600 drift. It would take a few minutes for the newly installed exhaust fans to pull out all the smoke and dust from the explosion, but those were precious minutes that could not be wasted. The crew quickly moved back into the drift, covering their mouths with their shirtsleeves in an attempt to filter out at least some of the dust being drawn into their lungs.

The dynamite had done its job—they had successfully punched through into the old drift beyond the dogleg. In the fog of smoke and dust, Sinclair could barely make out the failing timbers of the abandoned passageway beyond the rubble. He crawled across the pile of jagged greenstone and peered into the hazy corridor. He rubbed his eyes with the back of his hand, hoping that his vision had deceived him. The drift ahead was open for about 10 feet, then fully blocked by a cave-in.

"Son-of-a-bitch!" he yelled at the top of his lungs.

As the expletive echoed off the mine walls and slowly faded, it was punctuated by another sound—the unexpected and unmistakable rumble of another explosion.

"Where the hell did that come from?"

"Must've been an echo," one of the crew suggested.

"That was too late to be an echo," Sinclair replied. "And it was a single shot, not a round. Go down to the station and phone the surface. Tell them what we heard and see if they know where it came from. Tell them it sounded to me like it came from the Argonaut."

Lowell and Pickard were standing by the Kennedy head-frame when the top man answered the telephone and relayed the information to them directly. Lowell ran to the bureau truck and quickly drove across to the Argonaut. The crews working there had heard nothing unusual. The Argonaut foreman confirmed that no blasting had been used in firefighting efforts or for any other reason.

By the time Lowell made his way back to the Kennedy property, Pickard had assembled the members of the executive committee and other mining experts in the mine office to discuss this new development. If the explosion was not an echo and was not set off by Argonaut rescue crews, then it had to have come from deep within the Argonaut Mine. This led to two possible hypotheses—either the fire had ignited a store of dynamite, or the miners had set an explosion in order to communicate that they were still alive. According to Argonaut foreman Ben Sanguinetti, it was unlikely the fire had advanced far enough to reach a level where explosives were stored.

After careful consideration, the committee decided to proceed on the assumption that the blast came from the trapped miners. They ordered rescue crews on both levels of the Kennedy Mine to set off a single shot of explosives once each hour, then wait five minutes for an answer. They also assumed that if the Argonaut miners were alive, this regular blasting would let them know that a rescue attempt was in progress, which might improve their morale.

For additional input, the bureau again turned to their gadget guru, Lionel Duschak. At intervals throughout the day, work was temporarily halted so that Dr. Duschak could use the newest geophone to try to pick up any sounds coming from the Argonaut. An early cousin of the modern seismograph, a geophone could detect even the slightest sound vibrations coming from deep within the earth. Unfortunately, the distant rumbling of stamp mills at Jackson's many mines made Duschak's job extremely difficult. He reported no unusual or obvious sounds that could be linked to activities of the entombed men.

Could the trapped Argonaut miners survive for more than a week? Reporters put that question to California state mineralogist Fletcher Hamilton on September 6. "With good air and sufficient water, men should be able to live for two weeks or longer without starvation," he told them. Even though the miners had now been trapped for ten days, Hamilton was not alone in his optimism. Bureau of Mines district surgeon Dr. C. E. Kindall also bolstered hopes that the men could survive. "Never underestimate the human will to endure," he said. "Water is the key, and we believe there is plenty of drinkable water on the lower levels of the Argonaut."

Newspaper reporters jumped on the optimistic bandwagon, recalling the plight of California Edison employee Lindsey Hicks, who was trapped by a cave-in of the company's Current River tunnel in 1902 and survived for fifteen days. Even more relevant was the story of the 1909 Cherry Mine disaster in Illinois, during which twenty-two men lived for eight days on just water and the contents of a single lunch bucket. Cherry Mine officials believed that everyone still in the mine had perished, and it wasn't

Dr. L. H. Duschak, consulting engineer for the Industrial Accident Commission, analyzes gas samples from the Muldoon fan (left) and uses a geophone to listen for possible signals from the trapped miners (right).

until recovery efforts were under way that the twenty-two survivors were discovered behind a makeshift bulkhead.

The knowledge that Ernie Miller had survived the Granite Mountain fire continued to be a source of encouragement, even with the awareness that on that occasion he and his comrades were rescued after only four days. The common thread among survivors of mine fires was that they had successfully built bulkheads to keep out the smoke and carbon monoxide. If the Argonaut miners built such a bulkhead, if they chose a location close to the Kennedy workings where fresh air might be pulled through, if there was sufficient water to drink, and if they could endure the mental anguish of the ordeal, then some or all of the men might survive.

Additional cause for optimism came from Dr. Duschak's analysis of the air being drawn from the lower levels of the mine. If the men died in the first hours of the fire, as a number of experienced miners believed, their bodies would have achieved an advanced state of decay. One of Dr. Duschak's tests was designed to reveal gases associated with putrefaction of human tissue. The results of this test were consistently negative.

On Wednesday, September 6, news headlines changed from "Rescue Eminent" to "High Hopes for Rescue of Miners Dashed" when reporters learned of Bill Sinclair's discovery that the Kennedy 3600 beyond the new crosscut was fully caved. Experts now believed that the old drift was collapsed throughout its length. Rescue miners who had already invested nine days of the most backbreaking work they could imagine were completely demoralized. This would add at least five days to the effort of reopening the passageway to its original terminus after which they would still need to drive a diagonal raise to establish a connection with the Argonaut.

Three-quarters of a mile beneath the surface of the earth, the dedicated crews assigned to each of the rescue levels in the Kennedy Mine had come to be known as *36ers* or *39ers*, respectively, and a friendly competition was encouraged between them to boost spirits. The mines of Amador County came together to establish a reward of $5000 for the first crew to break through into the Argonaut.

On the 3600 level, 146 volunteers participated in the rescue effort, including relatives of trapped miners James Clayton, Ernie Miller, Peter Bagoye, Charles Fitzgerald, Mike Vujovich, Evan Ely, Lucio Gonzales, and others. Both Steve Pasalich and

Mitchell Jogo were 36ers for a time, as were several members of the Sanguinetti and Garbarini families.

Nineteen-year-old Elmer O'Berg was not among the rescue workers, although he would have done almost anything to join in the efforts to liberate his father and brother from their smoky tomb. "I'll sign any kind of paper so that you won't be responsible," he pleaded with the foreman. But the boy was noticeably ill, and mine officials knew that his only underground experience was four months in a mine in Goldfield, Nevada, where he was working when he received news of the Argonaut fire. Far more experienced miners had been refused membership in the exclusive 36er alliance of Kennedy and Argonaut regulars.

Tearing away at the muck-filled drift 300 feet deeper in the Kennedy Mine, the 39ers knew that they were stepchildren in the race to rescue the trapped miners. It was highly unlikely that any of the thirty-seven–man team would reach the Argonaut before workers punched through from the Kennedy 3600. Underground pressures had pushed the floor of the 3900 level up to within 1½ feet of the roof, and the mud was so sticky that two men were required for shoveling—one to shovel the muck and one to scrape the mud from the first man's shovel. On Thursday, September 7, a majority of the volunteers were prepared to quit, but most went back to work when informed of the $5000 bounty.

Maintaining the spirits of the rescue workers was a major challenge throughout the ordeal, and Mary Warrington realized that there could perhaps be no greater morale booster than to give the miners back something of great value that had been taken from them by the government. She obtained special dispensation from the federal Prohibition director in San Francisco to obtain 480 bottles of top-quality bourbon.

The whiskey was brought from San Francisco in two shipments. Clifford Durant, of Durant Motor Company in San Francisco, volunteered to drive one batch directly to the Argonaut. The second consignment was flown in by members of the U.S. Aviation Service stationed at the Presidio. Secured in a vault at the Amador County Bank and kept under strict control of the Red Cross, most of the booze was issued to workers on the 3600 and 3900 levels of the Kennedy Mine. A portion was also dispensed for medicinal purposes at the Red Cross hospital. The *drys* of Amador County, usually highly vocal on all affairs related to Prohibition, made no comment or complaint.

8 p.m., Saturday, September 9—Day 13

At the executive committee meeting held Saturday, September 9, it was suggested that battens be placed along the surface of the ground corresponding to the underground work so that the public could see how much progress was being made each day. This suggestion was not notable for its logic of purpose but for its unlikely source, Argonaut superintendent V. S. Garbarini. The plan was immediately approved and implemented.

Later that day, in order to counter a negative article in the *San Francisco Examiner,* the executive committee issued the following special press release as Bulletin No. 25:

> At a meeting of the executive committee . . . , attended by twelve, including the engineers and others in immediate charge of the rescue work, the question whether it was reasonable to suppose that any men remain alive in the mine was carefully considered.
>
> There are many points in the lower part of the mine where water entirely suitable for drinking can be obtained and it is believed that the men sought safety in parts of the mine where the air was good. The large majority of the entombed men were in excellent physical condition and, considering the fact that they have a

supply of water; it only remains to answer the question as to how long they can survive without food. As it was only twelve days at midnight September 8 since they had their last meal, it was the unanimous belief of those present that the men are still alive. No evidence to the contrary was offered by any of those present.

This statement is issued after long and careful discussion of the question and the Argonaut Manager is so confident the men are alive that a reward of $5000 has been offered to the first crew breaking into the Argonaut. The work on the 3600 and 3900 levels of the Kennedy Mine is being pushed at the utmost speed.

Signed: V. S. Garbarini, Chairman
E. C. Hutchinson
Fred L. Lowell, Secretary

As days turned into weeks, rescue crews, the press, and the community settled into a daily routine sustained by hopeful waiting. Ruth Finney began to wonder if there would ever be a climax to the Argonaut story.

"The September heat was intense," she recalled. "I was sunburned, and there was so much dust and grime everywhere that it didn't seem possible I would ever be clean again. But I hadn't been scooped; that was what counted."

She had lost all hope for a positive outcome. "I feel pretty sure the men are all dead," she wrote in her diary. "I want to have a good story for the climactic moment, when it comes, so today I decided I'd do it in advance, before I get so worn out I don't make sense."

In order to cover all possibilities, Ruth wrote two stories—one to be used if the trapped miners were brought out alive; another that would express the emotion of a failed rescue attempt. She wanted to base the latter article on the New Testament story of the resurrection of Christ. She felt that an analogy of the Argonaut breakthrough with the rolling away of the stone at Christ's tomb would be clever, and the religious angle would certainly be appropriate to the moment. Ruth remembered the story vaguely from her youth but needed to refer to a Bible to get the exact wording. To her surprise, the National Hotel did not provide Bibles in the room—in fact, there was not one Bible in the entire establishment.

"I started up one side of Jackson's main street and then down the other side searching for a Bible," Ruth recalled. "Everywhere I went, my queries brought only baffled stares. Finally, when I had almost given up hope, I went into a store that seemed to be selling nothing except guns. But when I told the owner what I wanted, he, to my incredulous delight, reached behind the racks of shotguns and the boxes of ammunition and produced a small New Testament."

Armed with her newly purchased Bible and a borrowed typewriter, Ruth wrote the two stories and mailed them to editor Harold Matson at the *Sacramento Star*. She had a feeling that the resurrection story was far more likely to be seen in print.

In addition to the *Sacramento Star* and United Press, Ruth was now contracted to Scripps-McRea's *San Francisco Daily News*, which sent two men to act as her assistants. She used one to drive copy to the telegraph office in downtown Jackson and the other to stand in line at the telephone office and call in late breaking news. Ruth's first loyalty was still to the *Star*, then to the United Press, and finally to the *Daily News*.

Ruth's primary competitor, the *San Francisco Examiner*, now had two editors and a staff of eighteen reporters and technicians in Jackson. Both the *Examiner* and the *Chronicle* had paid exorbitant fees to Pacific Telephone to run exclusive telegraph wires onto the Kennedy property, as well as additional telephone legs into downtown Jackson. The *Chronicle*'s telephone line terminated at the service station near the National

Hotel. The *Examiner's* phone was installed in the Garibaldi Saloon, which Frank Anderson of the *San Francisco Call* described as one of few places in town "that had at least heard of Prohibition."

Reporter O. K. Posey of the Sacramento *Union* saw it somewhat differently. "The Garibaldi Saloon was stocked with pre-Prohibition merchandise," he recalled, "and 1919 prices still prevailed. Some of the reporters from San Francisco, Chicago, and New York never had anything to drink but bathtub gin and jackass whiskey. The bartender could make all the old-time drinks, and took pride in them. I tell you, we had some sad days but some reasonably pleasant nights."

"When a correspondent cannot be reached at the mines or his hotel, he's at Garabaldi's," wrote another *Call* reporter, "and here the writers, cameramen, and operators are to be found during their idle moments relaxing from the terrible grind of today's biggest news story, and seeking a cool retreat from the temperature that daily runs considerably over 90 degrees."

Reporters who were not permanently ensconced at the mines continued to work the angle of the plight of the miners' families. In a little shack on Peak Hill, nearly a mile from the Argonaut Mine, Etta Nuttal Ely nursed her baby as her newly extended family sat around the dinner table. Her brothers, Joe and Floyd, had come from Arizona to work on the rescue crew. Their wives came to help with the Ely children and provide comfort to their sister-in-law. A celebratory dinner had been planned by *San Francisco Call* reporter Ernestine Black after hearing the previous day's optimistic news that a breakthrough was imminent. Steak and potatoes, elaborate fare for a miner's table, now sat untouched, and the *Call* reporter sat quietly analyzing the mood of the situation and plotting out her next sob-sister offering.

Miner Evan Ely came to Jackson from Globe, Arizona, in the early '20s with his wife, Etta, and three children. Their fourth child, Emma, was born just one month before the disaster.

"The babies have come so fast that we've never been able to save," Etta told Ernestine Black. "We were married down in my home in Arizona when Evan was working in the mines there. We came up here because Evan has folks here and he thought it would be good for the babies. He figured maybe he could get ahead and buy a ranch up here where the land is cheap someday. But how can a man save on $3.75 a day?"

In her article, Ernestine described the Elys' "rude three room shack with two inch gaps between some of the floor boards of unplaned wood." When a Sacramento store sent a new bed for the Elys, Etta turned it down. "What's the use?" she told Ernestine. "I can't sleep anyway. If Evan don't come out, I'll leave here and go back to Arizona with my brothers."

8 P.M., Thursday, September 14—Day 18

On September 14, Hugh Wolfin received a letter from A. J. Stinson, inspector of mines for the State of Nevada. The letter, a scathing rebuke of the firefighting and rescue methods used at the Argonaut, was also sent to various members of the press, giving Wolfin no chance to defend the bureau's actions before Stinson's comments were published. After giving a detailed analysis of the situation, Stinson's letter concluded:

The present plan of rescue through the Kennedy Mine could not result, when consummated, [in] reaching the entombed miners alive, on account of the necessary time consumed in drifting and crosscutting, which before pursuing such a plan could readily have been foreseen; but a greater reason exists militating against the probability of reaching the entombed miners alive; it is this, the methods you pursued in failing to downcast the Muldoon shaft and thereby upcasting the Argonaut shaft,

have resulted in forcing the fire and its noxious gases to
the lower level of the Argonaut Mine, where the miners
are entombed, with its resultant effect, particularly
since the Argonaut shaft has been bulkheaded at or
about the 2500 foot level above the fire.

Lastly, if due precautions are not taken before connection is made with the Argonaut shaft from the Kennedy Mine, such noxious gases in such lower levels of
the Argonaut Mine will pass through such connections
and the rescuing men may be fit subjects themselves for
rescue.

The letter was read in its entirety before the executive committee at their Friday morning meeting. There was no discussion of Stinson's analysis or accusations—the committee and
several dozen consultants had confirmed time and again that
the actions taken thus far were the only logical course. Their
concern was that the Nevada inspector would negate the optimistic disposition that the committee had worked so hard to
create. Tom Trebell was called into consultation, and a press
release was prepared by Lowell that once again detailed the
bureau's reasons for not shutting down or reversing the Muldoon fan. A week later, Wolfin would send a lengthy response to
Mr. Stinson, repudiating each of the inspector's points with facts
and opinions from the state's top mining engineers. Wolfin's letter concluded:

I believe that you must agree that when you outlined
the plan you submitted in your letter of September 13,
1922, you were not in possession of all the facts. If you
had had before you all of the available information, I
believe your decision would have been the same as that
of the other experienced mining men who considered

the problem. It is regrettable that you did not have all the available information before you gave your opinions to the press.

The committee had barely dispatched the Stinson affair when it was faced with yet another press-related issue that would compel them to take drastic measures. With every angle seemingly covered, the reporters had finally learned how to blend into the background and keep conflicts to a minimum— or so it seemed. Late Friday afternoon, as Ruth Finney conducted yet another interview with waiting relatives, she heard loud shouts coming from the direction of the Argonaut office. As she and other reporters hurried toward the disturbance, they were greeted by a small army of shotgun-toting sheriff's deputies. They were told they had five minutes to collect their belongings and leave the property or face jail time.

Within an hour, Jackson's main street was awash with complaining and confused reporters. It was well into the evening before Ruth learned that Robert Wilson, a reporter for the *San Francisco Examiner*, had erroneously reported that troops were being sent to the mine to take over rescue operations. After receiving a complaint from the executive committee, the *Examiner*'s managing editor recalled Wilson, but he refused to leave the property and had to be forcibly removed by Sheriff George Lucot. Wilson's wife and a newly arrived representative of the California governor's office stood by silently and watched as the reporter was taken away in handcuffs. The governor had previously advised mine owners that the state would not interfere if they decided to ban reporters from the property.

During an informal gathering at Garibaldi's Saloon, the journalists elected Ruth's good friend Tom Trebell to plead their case to the executive committee. Argonaut superintendent Garbarini refused to "waste his time arguing with reporters," and after he let his feelings be known in no uncertain terms, he left the matter to Fred Lowell. The normally easygoing Industrial Accident Commission engineer was firm in his resolve to permanently put an end to annoyances created by the press.

Lowell's first requirement was that the *San Francisco Examiner* print a retraction of the offending article, including an apology and notice that the author of the piece had been dismissed by the paper. Members of the press who wished to remain on the mine property would be required to sign a written agreement with stringent and explicit rules of conduct. Reporters who signed the agreement would be issued press cards that would allow them entrance to the property and a parking spot in a specified parking area. The Kennedy sawmill, which was within line of sight of the Kennedy shaft, would be converted for use as a press platform. Reporters would be required to remain on this platform and would agree not to approach mine employees or rescue personnel. The press would have to vacate the platform and the mine property each day no later than forty-five minutes past midnight.

Lowell asked Trebell to designate a committee of three, including himself, to act as liaison with the executive committee and speak on behalf of those signing the agreement. Trebell chose Ruth Finney and Ernest Hopkins of Universal News Service to serve with him.

Provided that all the reporters and photographers from every newspaper and wire service signed the agreement, the executive committee would, in consideration, increase the number and frequency of bulletins and provide notification of a breakthrough as soon as possible after it occurred, including the names of rescued men and/or recovered bodies. A single reporter selected by the others would be allowed to wait in the superintendent's office and carry news of important developments to the platform.

Argonaut superintendent Garbarini (right) watches as Amador County sheriff George Lucot tests a newly installed phone at the secured entrance to the Kennedy Mine property.

* * *

When Trebell returned to Garibaldi's, he carried a stack of over a hundred copies of the agreement, and he made it clear to the waiting reporters that this was the only way they would ever get back on the property of either mine. Although they grumbled and complained, everyone signed the agreement except for representatives of the *Sacramento Bee*.

When Trebell advised Lowell that one paper had refused to join the others, he fully expected that the ban on reporters would remain in place. But Lowell capitulated, with the very specific additional condition that no other paper would share information with *Bee* reporters or assist them in any manner.

The stance of the *Sacramento Bee* not to be "gagged" could not have been better news for Ruth Finney and the *Sacramento*

Star, which immediately flaunted their position as the only Sacramento paper with staff reporters on the scene. (The *Union,* recognizing the likelihood of a protracted climax, had long since recalled their reporter and was relying on AP wire communications.) Calling the *Bee* "Lilly White" and boldly printing the complete text of the "Jackson Treaty" on their front page, the *Star* reported that the agreement was simply a way to "gain an understanding with the mine and state officials as to where authentic news reports may be secured." The *Star* also pointed out that while the *Bee* announced that they would not allow their reporters to "sell out" the paper, they continued to print copy from wire services whose reporters had signed the agreement.

While ranting about the *Bee*'s grandstanding, the boastful *Star* gave a subtle hint of things to come: "[P]ending the rescue, from where else is a newspaper to learn what is going on nearly a mile underground? Send a reporter down? That would be a great reportorial achievement if it could be done—perhaps it has."

In a scathing (and somewhat colorful) editorial, the *Bee*'s publisher held his ground:

> The *Bee* does not care an infinitesimal twig from last's year's bird's nest if all the newspaper correspondents representing every press association on earth and all the other California newspapers signed that contract or not. Its representatives never will be permitted to sign it.
>
> Furthermore, no man or woman signed that contract with an idea of keeping it. There is not one of them who will not interview the workers and their wives at every chance they can get. They have signed this document probably because they think they can get rapid and first-hand news when the men or their corpses are found.

At the Kennedy Mine sawmill, converted for use as a press platform, reporter Ruth Finney talks on the phone (distant left) as her *Stockton Record* counterpart, Pearl Wright, works at a nearby desk.

And after they have gotten that from the mining company's reports, they will then turn around and interview the other side.

It took less than a day for reporters to become comfortably ensconced on the new press platform. Some staked a claim by building a makeshift desk on one corner or side of the open structure. Others simply sat on a bench or strolled about nervously. Reporters, cameramen, and telegraphers were all keyed up for the final flash of the discovery: when the Argonaut breakthrough would be announced and the question—too long unanswered—would finally be resolved.

Many of the small-town reporters felt that major San Francisco newspapers were given an unfair advantage by being allowed to extend telegraph wires to the platform for their exclusive use. The only other means of direct communication was a single telephone installed at the rear of the platform and restricted to incoming calls. Editors could call their reporters for updates at intervals throughout the day, but the reporters would have to drive to town and wait, as always, to make any outgoing phone calls.

As fate would have it, this arrangement would benefit Ruth Finney more than she could have possibly imagined.

CHAPTER 8

Undercover Work

12:30 A.M., Friday, September 15—Day 19

In the early morning darkness, Ruth Finney watched as a procession of scruffy miners in worn but freshly washed work clothes made their way from the change house to the collar of the Kennedy shaft. This was the morning relief crew for the 3600 level. One of the men—tall, raw-boned, and somewhat awkward—moved to the side of the path and nearly brushed up against Ruth as he passed. She looked down and saw a small piece of wadded paper on the ground. Taking great care not to attract attention, she bent down to straighten the buckle on her shoe and scooped up the paper. Minutes later, at the press platform, she unrolled it and read the words scrawled in pencil on its surface: "I have sold my body to the Argonaut Mine for rescue work. My shift is from one to seven in the morning. Pray for my soft hands."

With competition getting tougher by the day, *Star* editor Harold Matson had decided to try a bold and somewhat risky move. He sent one of his reporters to Jackson to pose as a miner and try to get work with the underground rescue crews. Other newspapers had tried the ruse and failed; a dirty face and some ragged clothes just weren't sufficient to turn a reporter into a miner. But *Star* reporter Irving Moore had always looked more like an outdoor laborer than a newspaperman. His awkwardness and his slow, country drawl concealed the fact that he was a well-educated and talented news writer.

"Let your whiskers grow," Matson told Moore on the day he left for Jackson. "There are reporters there who might recognize you. Avoid all acquaintances. But get down in the mine."

Moore knew nothing of mining or miners, but he knew that before he could even set foot on the mine property he needed to learn more about the work and the men who performed it. He took a motor stage from Sacramento to Martel, then walked down the hill past the mines to Jackson, stopping along the way for a drink at a roadhouse.

"I had heard that Amador County was decidedly wet," Moore remembered. "But I was given near beer. That was the only time during my stay in the county that I did not find the bartenders only too glad to serve the harder stuff. The drinks are plentiful, cheap, and easily obtained."

On his first day in Jackson, Moore met a couple of unemployed Italian tramp miners. He hung out with them in the speakeasies and walked the streets with them as they gave him a tour of the community. As evening approached, he was directed to an Italian boardinghouse in Jackson Gate, about a mile north of Jackson. "The Gate," as it was known locally, was a small village that occupied nearly the entire length of the narrow valley that lay just east of the Argonaut and Kennedy mines.

"It looked to me like Young Italy," Moore said. "No Americans were in evidence, and I began to wonder if the whole country was Italian."

At the boardinghouse, he enjoyed a meal of "nameless and unnamed Italian dishes," accompanied by a jug of homemade red wine. He then returned to Jackson under the cover of darkness. Nightfall would bring many of the reporters back to town, and Moore found himself darting into the shadows to avoid familiar faces. He finally scurried into a speakeasy that seemed to be filled entirely with miners but was thankfully devoid of reporters. Moore tried to strike up conversations with several different groups but was snubbed, he believed, because he was an unemployed tramp miner. Having accomplished little toward his goal, he returned to the boardinghouse in Jackson Gate.

As the night wore on, the owner of the boardinghouse, Julia, a rotund woman described by Moore as "four hundred pounds of vitality," served up a steady flow of red wine and strong opinions.

"Bradshaw—his fault," she told him in broken English. "He thought to lose skip so don't sent back for men. Bradshaw fool.

"I guess the government give mine bosses hell. Maybe no work for year, maybe two. No work, got to leave. Bad—bad for miners, no work."

Later, in his cramped and stifling little room, Moore planned to write down some of his thoughts about that first day in Jackson:

> The wine, the conversations, the strange atmosphere of the mining camp affected me strangely. Wild thoughts and fancies crowded through my brain. Now I was to write the epic of Jackson. I took pencil and paper— I rolled a cigarette—I stuck the pencil in my mouth. Then I went to bed. I had strange dreams. . . . I imagined thousands of wild animals crawling over me, eating on my flesh, tearing me to pieces, body and soul.

When Moore awoke the next morning, he found that he had not spent the night alone. His bedmates had been the miners' scourge since gold rush days—*Cimex lectularius*—blood-sucking bedbugs.

*   *   *

At breakfast, Moore sat alone and listened to the conversations around him.

"It's a mud hole," one miner said of the Kennedy Mine. "Hot as hell. It's a death trap. The Kennedy is worse than the Argonaut was. In Montana, the mines are different. There they got decent equipment. They have escape shafts. I'm going back to Montana."

The *Star* reporter spent his second day walking around the town, eavesdropping on the townspeople, especially the miners.

"Everybody disagreed, except on one point," he recalled. "I talked to miners, storekeepers, bartenders. All had given up hope of rescuing the men alive."

By the end of the day, he had picked up enough knowledge of mining to feel confident in going to the mines to ask for employment. The Argonaut foreman wasn't on the property, so he talked to the foreman at the Kennedy, who sent him back to the Argonaut. After waiting several hours to see the Argonaut boss—and dodging countless familiar faces—Moore was told to come back the next day.

As each day passed, it seemed that more and more recognizable faces lined the sidewalks of Jackson. While he was at the Argonaut Mine, Moore saw at least two dozen people who could identify him immediately. Most notable of these was Clarence Jarvis, the governor's personal representative at the disaster, whom Moore had interviewed on more than a few previous occasions. Jarvis, a member of the State Board of Control, was also a former county assessor for Amador County.

In order to avoid unwanted encounters, Moore decided to spend the daylight hours with the miners at the boardinghouse and only go onto the mine property at night, when most of the reporters were back in town. Twice more he met with the Argonaut foreman, and twice more he was told to come back later.

On his third day in Jackson, he decided to get up early and go to the mine, hoping to arrive before the grounds became crowded with the usual cast of players. As he reached the steps leading from the parking lot to the mine offices, he saw Clarence Jarvis step from one of the vehicles parked there. Moore ducked between two of the other cars parked in the lot and turned away from Jarvis, pretending to look down toward the Kennedy Mine. He carefully watched Jarvis's reflection in the car window, hoping that Jarvis would turn his back long enough for him to make his escape. Finally, Jarvis looked away for just a second. In that brief moment, Moore quickly moved past him and climbed the stairs to the mine. From the back, Moore looked like any of the dozens of volunteer miners who roamed the property.

Moore's luck alluding Jarvis was a harbinger of good things to come. As he approached the collar of the Argonaut, the foreman stepped out and confronted him.

"I was hoping you'd show up today. Found a place for you on the 1 A.M. shift if you want it."

Moore tried to temper his elation. A miner would be happy to get the work, but for a reporter it was the break of a lifetime. He gave the foreman a fake name for the time card.

"Report to Morovich, and don't be late. You can get a lamp and cap from the storeman."

Irving Moore had succeeded where many other newsmen had failed. He had been hired as a member of the rescue crew.

"The thought of entering the rescue hole filled me with awe, mixed with curiosity," he later wrote. "After tales I heard, there was also considerable fear. So I penned my note to the editor. The note was facetious, but contained the fact that I had secured a job."

Ruth Finney would be Moore's pipe to the outside world. Each day as he left the mine, she would wait near the path to

Looking south toward Jackson during rescue operations, a multitude of vehicles line the road below the Argonaut Mine.

the change room so that Moore could drop his wadded notes as he passed. These notes could contain only brief snippets of inside information. The major story would have to wait until he was safely back in Sacramento. "If they find out who you are," a colleague warned, "you will never come out of that shaft."

Late in the evening before his first shift, Moore found himself sitting alone in one of Jackson's hilltop cemeteries, contemplating the task before him.

"It was quiet there. Three days of constant dread lest someone should recognize me had been a strain. I wanted to be alone. It was good to just sit there and look at the moon and the dark outlines of the scrub oaks on the hills."

He thought of the forty-seven trapped men. "I tried to picture myself down there, weak from hunger, dazed by poisonous gas, lost to civilization, the beast, the elemental man with one thought, one idea—rescue. The picture was dim. I had no idea of the condition of a mine. But I was about to find out."

Moore arrived at the Kennedy at midnight, an hour before his shift, and picked up a cup of coffee at the Red Cross station. A fellow miner suggested that he "get a stick in it"—meaning to add a shot of whiskey. But Moore wanted to keep his mind sharp, and at that moment his thoughts were on the unknown adventure that awaited him three-quarters of a mile below the surface.

As he walked to the collar of the Kennedy shaft, he could see Ruth Finney standing near the path. He dared not look directly at her because other nearby reporters might recognize him. He adjusted his direction so that he would pass as closely as possible but kept his face turned away as he opened his hand and allowed the little wadded note to drop.

Minutes later, he was jammed into the Kennedy skip with nine other miners. Above the skip was a cage, and once the first group of miners was settled into the skip, planks were placed in the bottom of the cage so that more men could climb aboard. Unlike the inclined Argonaut shaft, the Kennedy shaft was perfectly vertical, facilitating a high-speed descent. In his article for the *Star*, Moore described the drop into the mine:

Two bells! The big drum on which the cable was coiled began to move slowly, then faster and faster. We were below the surface, traveling downward at the rate of an express train. Nobody spoke. Water dripping from the shaft splashed and spattered over us. From the second we left the surface the air changed, the world below was so different. We seemed to be engulfed in an incomprehensible something which was not air, yet which beat on

The headframe of the fully vertical Kennedy Mine shaft.

our ears like the crashing of thunder. My ears pained. I thought the drums would burst. . . . I wanted to yell. But I stood there like the others, silent, hands hanging.

"That was the 3500 foot level." One of the miners had spoken in a detached faraway voice. It surprised me that I could hear at all. . . . A scraping of feet over our heads. The skip came to a jarring stop, bobbed up and down like a toy balloon and stopped 3600 feet below the surface of the earth.

Moore was assigned to a work crew consisting of twenty men. He and several others were stationed at 150-foot intervals along the 3600 drift. His assignment seemed simple: He would wait at his station until a man arrived with a wheelbarrow full of muck. He would then take it to the next station, pass it on to the man there, and return with an empty wheelbarrow. His shift would last for only thirty minutes, then he would rest at the main station for one hour before returning to work—four shifts of thirty minutes, four hours of rest.

As he followed the rest of the crew down the passageway, it seemed at first exactly as he had imagined it—straight, wide, with regular sets of timbering. But then they reached the area that had once been caved in and was now reopened.

> I found it as crooked as a mountain goat trail, and as rough. It began to get lower. I had to double up, bending back and legs to keep from striking the jagged timbers overhead. Hot and stifling! Sweat was pouring off my body in streams. The absence of oxygen in the air made breathing difficult. Already I felt weak and sick. . . .
> I pictured myself being carried out unconscious.

In standard mining practice, as the face of a drift was pushed forward, rails for the ore carts were laid in place to facilitate removal of waste rock. During the rescue operation, however, the laying of rails was considered too time-consuming. Therefore, the backbreaking job of rock removal was done with wheelbarrows pushed along a pathway of wooden planks. There was still 32 feet of drift to be cleaned out before the 36ers reached the point where they would start a 77-foot rise to connect with the Argonaut.

Looking down the drift from his assigned station, which was several hundred feet from the active face of the drift, Moore could see the bobbing light of an approaching miner. Without a word, the miner dropped the handles of his wheelbarrow, grabbed the empty one, and silently wheeled away, back down the drift. Now it was Moore's turn.

Miners working the Kennedy 3600 rescue drift prepare to be lowered into the Kennedy shaft.

I took hold of the barrow. My hands slipped on the muddy handles. A few feet and the wheel missed the planks, which were submerged in the slushy slime. About 150 feet to the next station. Finally I got there. [The miner there] took my full barrow; I took his empty and started back. At my station a full barrow was waiting. Then I realized why the men only worked in half-hour shifts. . . . Blindly I wheeled barrows back and forth. I was filled with a great desire to fall flat in the muck. I was no longer a man. A beast propelled by sight of the barrows and vague knowledge that they must be wheeled.

Finally, the end of the half hour came. I could scarcely crawl back to the station and rest. . . . I fell flat on my back, breathing the foul gas-filled air in an attempt to get back my breath.

The other miners noticed Moore's instability, but they assumed he had a hangover, and he played along with the assumption. They joked about his condition, which gave Moore some solace. After all, he still had some pride left. He would rather have them think he was hung over than know that he was unable to do what they considered a man's work.

After stumbling through the narrow confines of the drift, the expanse of the 3600 station seemed almost cathedral-like. Even the damp air, with its ever-present metallic smell and taste, was a revitalizing change from the gas-filled workings. As the rescue workers sat around and talked, Moore tried to concentrate on the details of the conversations. He was there for the story, and what these men had to say was an important part of that story. They talked about girls. They talked of the perils of coming to work drunk or hungover. They talked about the female reporters they had seen in town. They talked about what they would like to do to the newspapermen—which did little to settle Moore's anxiety. They talked about how much they hated working in the mines. And then they returned to the subject of girls. No one mentioned the trapped men or the rescue effort.

"Ten minutes more," one of the men announced after glancing at his pocket watch. The other miners began filling their lamps with water and carbide. Moore could barely make it across the station to the water barrel. He later said that it was like walking on the deck of a small ship rolling in a high sea.

During the next shift, Moore would get to see the face of the drift, where nature's reclamation of the Kennedy 3600 drift still challenged the miners' picks. But what he had to do to get there

Working undercover as a rescue miner, *Sacramento Star* reporter Irving Moore ran wheelbarrows loaded with mud and waste rock through the narrow confines of the Kennedy 3600 rescue drift.

almost did him in. He and others of the crew were called upon to bring in a new set of timbers from the station.

> I struggled along behind the others with my timber. I was glad to be behind so the others could not see how I staggered, falling against the sides of the drift, then regaining my balance. . . . All the life seemed to be gone out of my legs. . . . Panting, nearly exhausted, I got to the end of the drift, where the men's shovels were biting into the barrier yet separating the Kennedy from the Argonaut.

No sooner had he dropped his timber than he was ordered back to the barrow brigade.

I dreaded to see the miner's lamp which would tell me that it was coming. . . . I hated that man for bringing me a loaded wheel barrow. I was no longer a man. I was an unthinking beast, in desperation. Yet I could not quit. I must get those wheel barrows moved to the next station. . . . My only thought—when will relief come?

When his second shift ended, Moore literally crawled on hands and feet most of the way back to the station. With mud and sweat pouring down his face and body, he lay down on a narrow plank, closed his eyes, and panted like a dog. He wanted to quit. He thought about how easy it would be to simply say he was too sick to continue, then catch the next skip up to fresh air and a soft bed. He would gladly share his cot with hungry bedbugs. At that moment, there was little satisfaction at being the first and only reporter to work on the rescue crew.

Moore watched as the other miners stuffed grapes, peaches, and pears into their mouths from the basket that had been sent down by the Red Cross. They ate with their black, mucky hands, unconcerned that they were eating nearly as much dirt as fruit. Food was the farthest thing from Irving Moore's mind. He simply wanted to rest for as long as they would let him.

But suddenly his attention was caught by a nearby conversation. For the first time, some of the men began to talk about the trapped Argonaut miners who were the objective of their wearisome labor.

"When we get these birds out, I'm through," said the big Irishman.

"It's all a waste," said the little Dutchman. "They're all dead."

The others nodded in agreement, and the conversation quickly turned to their favorite subject—girls.

Someone had taken his pocket watch out and hung it from a nail on one of the central timbers of the station so that everyone could see the time. Every time Moore opened his eyes, another fifteen minutes had passed. Then came the dreaded prompt: "Five minutes—fill your lamps."

> I don't know how that next shift passed. I scarcely remember except that I wheeled and wheeled—always wheeling in the mucky low drifts, falling from side to side, getting to the end of my run, somehow. Conscious of one thought, my relief. . . . Then rest again . . . until I would again be at work, hoping desperately for seven o'clock and final relief.

By the end of the third shift, Moore did not stand out so much from the other members of the crew. They too were feeling the effects of the strenuous labor. During the final break, most of the men sat silently watching the minutes tick away. Then it was time for the last leg.

> The thought of being through when this shift was over encouraged me. I must stand it now, I thought.
> Then, the last shift was over. We returned to the shaft and took the trip in the skip. I remember little of it except as a bad dream.
> It was over. Again I was in the open air. I made a firm resolve that I would never go underground again for man, devil, or gold.

During Moore's six-hour shift, the face of the Kennedy 3600 rescue drift had advanced about 8 feet. An additional 24 feet, and they could begin blasting out the 77-foot raise that would finally connect the two mines.

Although he had planned to spend several days as a member of the rescue crew, one day in the mine was more than enough for

Irving Moore. He returned to Sacramento and wrote a feature article that would be held in reserve by the *Star* until the fate of the Argonaut miners was known.

Moore was out of the mine, but he was not out of danger. After his story appeared as a series in three issues of the newspaper, several threatening calls were received at the *Star* offices. The men with whom Moore had associated during his stay in Jackson resented that he had gotten away with his deceptive plan and vowed to get him. Sacramento police were advised of the threat, and the *Sacramento Star* building was placed under armed guard.

CHAPTER 9

Breakthrough

On Friday, September 15, with 12 feet of hard-packed muck remaining to be extracted from the Kennedy 3600 drift, the executive committee decided to discontinue the work of clearing the old passageway and start the diagonal raise that would finally connect the two mines. The bureau's consulting engineers had concluded that driving the raise through virgin rock would take no more time or effort than clearing the remainder of the old drift, and an early start on the raise would achieve a net gain of 6 feet. Starting early would also slightly reduce the angle of the raise, making it easier to move men and machinery through it once it was completed.

7 A.M., Saturday, September 16—Day 20

By Saturday morning, 19 feet of the raise had been blasted out, but a new problem had presented itself. Each round of blasting produced a significant amount of smoke, and although electric fans had been installed in the drift to help clear out the smoke and dust, there was a minimum delay of fifteen minutes before crews could get into the end of the drift and remove the rubble. This limited blasting to a maximum of two rounds during each thirty-minute shift.

Later that morning, in anticipation of the eventual breakthrough, the headquarters for the executive committee was transferred from the Argonaut to the Kennedy. After being informed of the lack of overnight progress, the committee asked Kennedy Mine president E. C. Hutchinson to hold a meeting with his foreman, Bill Sinclair.

"We know you and your boys have put your all into this effort, Bill. And we know how much you want to finish it out," Hutchinson told him. "But *you* know it's taken a whole lot longer than anyone expected. That's not your fault. Now we need to pick up the pace. We're going to send down apparatus crews to finish the work. They won't have to wait for the smoke to clear, and we can add at least one more round of blasting per shift."

Sinclair stared at his boss and bit his lip, then decided not to hold his tongue. "You expect me to go down there and tell the men they're not gonna be the ones to punch through?" he asked incredulously. "You better be prepared to bring in troops to pull 'em out, then have a strong cage ready to lock 'em in. You know this was never about the work—and it's sure as hell not about any reward. It's the breakthrough that counts—that's what they're down there for. And now you want to take that away from them?

"You want three rounds per shift, we'll give you three rounds per shift. Hell, we've been breathin' gas for three weeks— a little powder smoke ain't gonna kill us any quicker. You want a breakthrough tomorrow night? We'll break through tomorrow night. But let us do the work. Don't bring in outsiders."

This was exactly the reaction Hutchinson had anticipated. "I can't order you or the men to take that risk, Bill. But any man that knows the danger and still wants to continue under the new schedule can do so. We'll hold off on using apparatus men until we see if you can step up the pace. But if anybody gets sick or hurt, or if we see that it's taking too long, I'll expect you and the boys to make way. If there's any chance left at all to bring those men out alive, we have to move fast."

Minutes later, Sinclair sat with the relief crew at the 3600 station and explained the situation. He made it clear that anyone who was worried about his personal health or safety could back out with no hard feelings. Not one miner left the station. The same option was given to every shift that worked during the next twenty-four hours. Every man on every crew remained.

After every blast, the miners ran back into the drift with handkerchiefs tied over their mouths and began loading muck into the wheelbarrows. Each man carried a flask of vinegar, the miner's cure for a powder gas headache. Up in the murky raise, with acrid smoke burning their eyes and lungs, the drillers blindly bored holes for the next round. Each blast advanced the face of the raise by a little more than 1 foot.

7 A.M., Sunday, September 17—Day 21

By Sunday morning, the crews had moved the raise upward 30 feet, leaving 30 feet more to be drilled and blasted before a connection could be made with the Argonaut. Barring unforeseen delays, they would just make Hutchinson's midnight deadline.

On the surface, at the Kennedy Mine, the executive committee was busy laying out two alternative plans—one for rescue, one for recovery. Complete control of both these efforts would be given to Bureau of Mines district engineer Byron Pickard.

A large rescue station was established near the collar of the Kennedy shaft, with a stack of fifty canvas stretchers forming a short wall along one perimeter. Mounds of blankets and miscellaneous first aid equipment were organized by a team of nurses who were brought in from nearby hospitals by the Industrial Accident Commission. Surgeon-miner C. E. Kindall and Jackson area doctor E. E. Endicott were placed in charge of under-

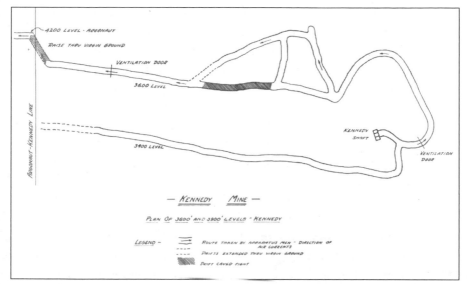

A map of the Kennedy 3600 and 3900 rescue drifts taken from the official report of Bureau of Mines district engineer Byron Pickard.

ground first aid efforts. As part of their preparation, the two physicians ordered a milk truck to be parked nearby, filled with ice to keep milk and other perishables cool in the late summer heat. For the starving and dehydrated men, small amounts of milk and broth would be the best first meal.

Knowing that members of the crews who drove the 3600 and 3900 rescue drifts were anxious to be a part of rescue efforts, a plan was devised using apparatus men to transport any rescued Argonaut miners as far as the Kennedy drift, after which teams of fresh air men—selected from 3600 and 3900 mining crews—would take over and bring the rescued men to the surface. These crews would remain under the supervision of Bill Sinclair and Doc Murphy. Once ventilation had been restored to the Argonaut, these workers could also be used as relief for the apparatus men.

Everyone trained in the use of the Gibbs apparatus would be deployed in initial underground rescue and recovery efforts. These men were divided into three groups of two teams each, designated as group A, teams 1 and 2; group B, teams 1 and 2; and group C, teams 1 and 2. The most experienced Bureau of Mines and IAC personnel would act as team captains. Team A1, made up of those who were highly trained in first aid procedures, would be the first to enter the Argonaut Mine once a connection had been established. Rodney Hecox would serve as team captain.

Rescue and firefighting efforts had severely depleted the cache of canaries that had been secured through typical sources. After a connection with the Argonaut was secured, having a supply of these birds to test the level of gas in the mine was essential. Through newspapers and the local grapevine, a request was put out to the women of Amador County to donate their canaries to the cause. By nightfall, cages filled to overflowing with little yellow birds were being attended by Red Cross volunteers at the Kennedy Mine.

Meanwhile, the Argonaut Mine property was nearly deserted. The miners' families had long since returned to their homes and rescue personnel had all been transferred to the Kennedy. Four volunteer apparatus men were assigned to keep watch over the bulkhead that sealed the Argonaut shaft to assure that the upper limit of the fire did not rekindle.

As midnight approached, 11 feet of greenstone remained between the Kennedy 3600 raise and the Argonaut 4200 crosscut. Sinclair suggested that a series of two or three test holes be drilled with a 12-foot extension bit to determine whether there was a danger of carbon monoxide being drawn or pushed back into the Kennedy workings. Two airtight doors were installed in the Kennedy 3600 drift to restrict airflow. With a pair of oxygen masks nearby and a caged canary waiting to test the air, drillers Thomas Penrose and Ray Dumont worked together and

Jackson area resident Ruth Jones, age 4, donates her pet
canary for use in the rescue effort.

in relief of one another to bore the first hole. A team of apparatus men waited at the base of the raise to relay progress reports. All other personnel would remain outside the closed doors.

Drilling the long hole was tedious and time-consuming, and
the air in the sealed-off end of the drift was quickly getting
stale. The temperature at the face of the raise was above 100
degrees F. In order to cool the drill bit and reduce hazardous
rock dust, the drill (called a jack) was designed so that water
passed through the center of the long extension (called a drill

steel) and out a hole in the tip of the bit. This water gushed back on the drillers and spilled down the incline, making the floor slick and degrading the stability of the passageway. As the drill progressed farther into the rock, the two men had to regularly stop and move the jack up the slippery incline, then wedge it firmly in place before continuing. If their calculations were correct, based on the length of the drill steel, the collar of the jack would be nearly in contact with the face of the raise when the bit broke through the floor of the Argonaut 4200 crosscut.

3 A.M., Monday, September 18—Day 22

At three o'clock Monday morning, the drill steel lost its bite and began spinning wildly, indicating that it no longer had resistance. About 2 feet of steel remained between the jack collar and the face of the raise. The engineers' estimate had been off by less than a foot. When the drill was removed, air gushed outward through the tiny hole from the Kennedy to the Argonaut with such force that it extinguished the workers' carbide lamps. There was no need to reach for the gas mask or the canary. As Garbarini had predicted, the Muldoon fan was still pulling air out of the Argonaut lower levels.

Unable to relight their lamps due to the strong movement of air, Penrose and Dumont slid back down the raise to the floor of the drift where the team of apparatus men had already switched to battery-powered flashlights. The group then made their way back to the first sealed door. It took four men working from both sides to get the door open, after which it quickly snapped shut from the suction.

When V. S. Garbarini received word that the graveyard shift had punched a hole through to the Argonaut, he immediately called down to the 3600 station, asking them to hold off on shooting any further rounds of explosives until he could inspect the raise. But in the time it took for his message to reach the crew, blasters had already detonated the final round and were working to clear the resulting pile of rubble.

When Garbarini was informed that a round had already been shot, he gave orders that no one was to go back into the raise until he had made a personal inspection of the conditions. At 3:40 A.M., Garbarini and the bureau's superintendent of fresh air crews, C. H. Fry, made their way into the Kennedy 3600 raise and verified the strong movement of air into the Argonaut. They then returned to the surface and informed Dr. Duschak, who went immediately to the Muldoon shaft and took new readings of the air being exhausted by the fan. He reported that the air had increased in both volume and quality. Everyone now knew that the climax of this long and tortuous saga was near.

For twenty-one days, the world had waited to learn the fate of the forty-seven trapped miners. Now, telegraph and teletype operators, newspaper pressmen, photographers, and motion picture cameramen were poised to broadcast the climactic news. In a small room on the top floor of the Hale Brothers Department Store in San Francisco, a truly exceptional event was about to take place. For the first time in its history, the *San Francisco Call* would deliver a wireless newspaper.

For the fledgling radio industry, 1922 was a banner year. The hundreds of amateur stations that had been vying for airtime were slowly becoming supplanted by commercial enterprises, prompting the Department of Commerce to require all nongovernment stations to obtain a limited commercial license. All of these stations broadcast on the single authorized frequency of 833 kHz, requiring neighboring stations to agree on a time-sharing schedule.

On Friday, September 15, 1922, the *Call* announced that it would use its scheduled twice daily airtime to broadcast on-the-spot news being received by telegraph from its correspondent at

At the collar of the Kennedy shaft, rescue crews prepare to enter the Argonaut Mine via the newly completed Kennedy rescue drift.

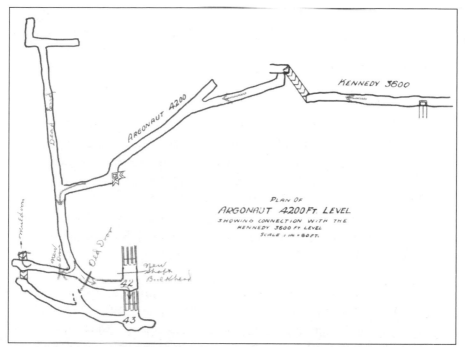

From the Bureau of Mines official report, a map of the Argonaut 4200 drift and crosscut showing the connecting raise from the Kennedy 3600 rescue drift.

the Kennedy Mine. "Hundreds of persons, including seamen and rangers and others who are separated from civilization, will be enabled to pick up the latest happenings at the mine," the newspaper announced. According to the *Call*, thousands within a radius of 1000 miles would be able to receive last-minute news of the rescue work.

Because radio was still a two-way medium, each broadcast began with the transmission, "Hello, hello—this is radio station KPO broadcasting from Hale Brothers Department Store for the *San Francisco Call*. Receivers will kindly give us a check."

The *Sacramento Star* was the only newspaper to claim that it received reports directly from Jackson by radio. On Saturday,

Ruth Finney had advised her editor that a breakthrough was imminent, and Matson brought his full staff into the office in anticipation of putting out an extra. In her diary, Ruth mentions that Matson sent her a shortwave radio by which she could reach the *Star* if all other means failed. Although Ruth never mentioned using the radio, several of her articles appeared in the newspaper with the subheading "By Radio to the *Star.*"

Fred Lowell's Saturday bulletin indicated that the end was near, and newspeople were allowed to stay on the Kennedy property later than usual in anticipation of the breakthrough. But by 1 A.M. on Sunday morning, it had become clear that nothing significant was going to happen until the next day, and the reporters were escorted off the property with a promise that they would be notified immediately should a breaking story present itself.

That morning, on her way back to her room at the National Hotel, Ruth waited in a long line at the phone office to call Matson and let him know that he could send everybody home. The anticipation of the impending finale kept her awake most of the night, and she spent her time reading stories in competitive newspapers and writing in her diary.

"I'm still in charge of the story of UP, *[Daily] News*, and *Star*, and am sending feature stories to NEA as well," she wrote. "Getting huge front page bylines. It has been the most thrilling experience of my life and I have learned more about newspaper work than I ever dreamed of. The whole thing is hell for almost everyone else involved, but for me, it's something I wouldn't have missed."

6:30 A.M., Monday, September 18—Day 22

Ruth returned to the press platform Monday morning after having gotten about two hours of sleep. Upon her arrival at the Kennedy Mine, she was given bulletins No. 36 and 37:

5 A.M.—The last blast shattered the intervening rock between the raise and the 4200 level of the Argonaut Mine to such an extent that air was being sucked through from the Kennedy Mine to the Argonaut Mine through a crack in sufficient quantities that it would extinguish a miner's light. The face of the raise measured 72 feet from the drift. It will take a few hours in order to bar down and make an opening large enough for men to pass through.

5:23 A.M.—Nothing new; can't get up in raise until muck is cleared out.

6:10 A.M.—Sixteen-inch hole through into Argonaut; gas, powder smoke going that way; doors kept closed; asked that Argonaut compressor be stopped.

According to Dr. Duschak, the volume of air being exhausted by the Muldoon fan increased fourfold after the Kennedy/Argonaut connection was made, yet there was no increase in smoke or carbon monoxide levels. This was promising news on two fronts: If the lower limit of the fire in the Argonaut shaft was still active, the increase in airflow would certainly have fed the flames and increased the volume of smoke. Also, if the lower levels of the mine were filled with carbon monoxide, there should have been a spike in CO readings when the gas was flushed out by the sudden flow of fresh air. Tests for gases from human putrefaction also continued to show negative.

Throughout the morning, crews worked to enlarge the opening in the floor of the Argonaut 4200 crosscut and install supporting timbers in the raise so that rescue teams could safely pass between the two mines. The rescue miners continued to have trouble keeping their lamps lit due to the strong flow of air into the Argonaut. The executive committee decided that it was important to keep the Muldoon fan running at full speed in order to clear out as much smoke and gas as possible before rescue teams entered the Argonaut.

Until they were able to inspect the Argonaut shaft, the committee also wanted to keep all their options open, so they asked the miners working on the Kennedy 3900 drift to continue to push ahead. There was always the possibility that falling debris had blocked the Argonaut shaft at or below the 4200 level, in which case a lower connection would be needed. At 11 A.M., two men entered the Argonaut Mine from the Kennedy raise and began clearing the drift in preparation of the arrival of rescue team A1.

At about noon, Byron Pickard descended into the Kennedy Mine and made his way through the narrow 3600 drift to the newly completed connection. He described his initial trek in a report to the bureau:

> One had to travel some 2000 feet where in places the back was not over 2.5 to 3 feet high. The workings were very hot and uncomfortable. At the end of this winding passage there was an incline raise, inclined about forty-five degrees, which had been hastily driven and as a consequence the back was low and the area restricted. There were no ladderways in the raise, it being necessary to climb up the timbers with the aid of a rope. Water was running down and the floor was slippery and muddy. To get through to the Argonaut 4200 from the crosscut which had connected at the mouth of the raise, it was necessary to crawl through a very small opening as no time was taken to retimber it or put it into shape. Very little timbering had been done in the raise, and as a consequence there were a number of narrow escapes from falling rock.

Accompanied by V. S. Garbarini and selected members of apparatus team A1, Pickard explored the Argonaut 4200 crosscut and drift up to the ventilation door that separated the drift from the 4200 station. This was the area that Garbarini had hoped the men had chosen for sanctuary. There was no evidence that anyone had been in the crosscut for some time. They then opened the ventilation door and stepped out into the 4200 station. There was the strong odor of smoke, but the caged canary that accompanied them showed no signs of distress.

While Pickard and other members of the team prepared the 4200 station for use as a fresh air base, Hecox and Sanguinetti explored the remainder of the 4200 drift to its terminus at the ventilation raise to the Muldoon shaft. At 1:00 P.M., they returned to the station and reported finding nothing out of the ordinary. The drift was filled with the odor of smoke, but their canary seemed to suffer no ill effects. The balance of apparatus crew A1 and all of back up crew A2 had arrived at the station and were preparing for an all-out search.

Before anyone was allowed to go down to the lower levels, Pickard wanted to make sure they would be safe from any debris that might fall down the shaft from the fire zone above. He ordered a fresh air crew to build a bulkhead across the shaft just above the 4200 station. This bulkhead took two hours to complete, during which time the apparatus teams laid out a search plan and devised a method of communicating with the fresh air station by tapping on the pipes that ran through the manway portion of the main shaft.

4:20 P.M., Monday, September 18—Day 22

Wearing Gibbs apparatus and goggles, Rodney Hecox and team A1 moved down the manway ladder to the 4350 level. As they reached the 4350 station, a canary being carried by one member of the team began to show signs of distress, and in less than a minute the bird expired. Hecox swung himself back onto the manway ladder and signaled the fresh air station—one

Miners enter the Argonaut 4200 crosscut from the Kennedy 3600 raise.

tap on the water pipe, then two taps, indicating they had arrived at the station; then two taps followed by four taps, indicating bad air. The team then began to search the 4350 drift.

Several hundred feet into the drift, crew members found the ventilation door still tightly closed. They propped the door open, allowing fresh air to rush into the passageway. Then the crew made their way to the end of the drift and carefully examined the ladder in the ventilation raise that led to the Muldoon shaft. Seeing no mud on the rungs or other indications that anyone had used the ladder, they began to retrace their steps back to the station.

When team A1 arrived back at the main shaft, they found rescue team A2 waiting in relief. The opening of the 4350 ventilation door had cleared the air in the station and the men were able to remove their air masks and goggles. Hecox suggested that the second team bring a canary and help them explore the 4350 crosscut that branched off the drift about 200 feet in from the station. That would complete their search of the 4350 level, and team A2 could then proceed down to the 4500 while the first team took a break. It was now 4:20 in the afternoon on the twenty-second day after the discovery of the fire.

As the teams entered the crosscut, their canary immediately began to show signs of distress. The air in the passageway was hazy, indicating that this crosscut was not affected by the improved ventilation of the 4350 drift. The beams of a dozen carbide lamps danced off the walls and ceiling as the team searched for any sign that the trapped miners might have passed that way. About 50 feet into the crosscut, all lamps were directed forward as each of the team members caught sight of the barrier that blocked their way. A perfectly constructed bulkhead of stacked rock sealed off the end of the crosscut.

Hecox quickly looked at the canary. It lay lifeless on the floor of the wooden cage. He then pulled out the small hammer he had used to signal the fresh air station and approached the wall. He tapped three quick, distinctive taps, then paused and tapped three times again. The sound of air moving through his oxygen mask now seemed a vociferous roar. He quickly held his breath and shut off the main valve. The rest of the team followed his lead. Once again he tapped three quick taps and listened intently for a reply. With everyone holding their breath and standing perfectly still, the eerie silence was deafening.

Hecox opened the valve on his oxygen tank and took a deep breath. Some of the men began coughing as they struggled to regain normal respiration. One of the men rushed forward and began ripping rocks from the wall, and others joined in. Hecox tried to pull them back, but the rescue team had become an uncontrollable mob, possessed by the need to see what lay beyond the bulkhead.

*　*　*

At the 4200 fresh air station, Byron Pickard was helping Dr. Kindall arrange his medical supplies when Rodney Hecox and the rescue teams stepped from the manway ladder onto the station floor. All of the men looked extremely tired and dejected.

"They built a bulkhead in the 43 crosscut," Hecox reported to Pickard as he sat down on a stack of blankets. "It was a beautiful piece of work. They even chinked the cracks with bits of their clothing soaked in mud. The air in front of it was foul and I wanted to wait until it was clear, but the men got a little anxious and tore it down. There's a second bulkhead about 25 feet farther in, but the air in between is really bad. I tapped on the wall and didn't get any answer, and I told the men to wait until we can clear out the gas before we go any farther. If there's anybody alive back there, we don't want to bring the gas in on them."

"You did the right thing, Rod," Pickard replied. "I've got teams working on bringing phone and electricity through, and we still have to do additional shoring up of the raise. You look done-in. Why don't you go up and tell Wolfin and the others what you found, then get some relief. Take both these teams with you and send down B1 and B2."

With Hecox on his way to the surface, Pickard and Kindall donned Gibbs apparatus and made their way down the ladder to the 4350 level. Pickard wanted to make a close inspection of the 4350 crosscut before they dismantled the second bulkhead. He saw that the passageway was equipped with a compressed air pipe and sent word back to the fresh air station to have crews attach the Argonaut main pipe to the active Kennedy 3600 compressed air line so that fresh air could be blown into the drift to clear out the bad air more quickly.

At the face of the second bulkhead, Pickard couldn't resist the temptation to call out, hoping for any answering sound that might indicate someone was alive on the other side. His voice echoed against the crosscut walls and the vibrations brought down a small rock from the upper right corner of the barricade. Pickard glanced up to see where it came from. His shoulders dropped and he gave out a moan of disappointment. There was a gaping hole in the wall near the roof of the crosscut. The second bulkhead was unfinished.

When the miners who broke through into the Argonaut returned to the surface, the reporters crowded along the edge of the platform to watch them exit the shaft. Perhaps they expected something of a victory parade, or at least a cheer of triumph, with caps being flung in the air. Instead, the 36ers climbed from the skips and walked lethargically toward the change house. A reporter from the *San Francisco Call* shouted to a straggler, "Did the men go wild with excitement when they knew at last they were through?"

The man walked nearer the platform and paused for a minute.

"We expected to get through. There was no excitement, but the air sucked down through the shaft so that our hats blew off and our lights went out."

"But you've won," said the reporter energetically. "Do you think some of them are alive?"

The man's eyes narrowed and he shrugged his shoulders and walked on toward the change house door.

The reporter turned to one of his associates. "Why would they work so hard just so someone could go in and sew bodies into canvas sacks?" he asked incredulously.

"There had to be a spark of hope," his colleague answered. "Surely they believed there might be just one still alive."

His enthusiasm dulled by the miner's dismal mien, the *Call* reporter sat down at his makeshift desk and began to type. As the bright summer sun slowly sank behind the hills, his emotions poured forth in words that captured the moment with near perfection:

> The shaft of the Argonaut looks like some monstrous tombstone; and there bites into the mind, with a sickening terror, the picture of men suddenly caught down there in the depths; suddenly and with a ghastly agony realizing their dooms; rushing through the impenetrable dark of the tunnels, seizing one another mute with panic. Then, the dull frightful veiling of hours that belong not to the day or night, but to a shrouding misery.
>
> And now, this last night of waiting, of heart breaking hope begins. In a moment everyone who may is in an automobile speeding past hills and hollows on the ten minute ride to the shaft of the Kennedy. Darkness begins to settle. A great yellow light gleams high in the sky. It is the light on the shaft of the Argonaut. The light hangs there and glows and the shaft seems now a beacon—never a tomb.
>
> For in the cathedral hush of this Indian summer evening, when stars are coming out and it is sweet to live, there comes fresh and incredible, the frightening thought, "Men are buried here alive. They're waiting. Oh, this may be the very last moment of endurance. Even now, the last torturing breath may pass. Hurry—hurry—"

CHAPTER 10

The Hand of Fate

Amid the chaos and tumult, the planned paving of Jackson's Main Street was completed on September 18 right on schedule. For as long as anyone could remember, the downtown thoroughfare had been composed of dust and gravel in the summer and mud and gravel in the winter. The hooves of tens of thousands of horses, mules, and oxen, and the wheels of as many wagons and stagecoaches, had kept Jackson sheathed in a dusty coat for three-quarters of a century. The arrival of a smooth, black, oiled surface with neatly painted white lines marking slots for parking was no minor transfiguration. The town would never again be the same.

Call reporter Ernestine Black wrote:

Main Street Jackson has been wiped out. The main street that brought Hobart Bosworth, Will Rogers, and other motion picture stars here to stage street scenes in the quaint, up-ended thoroughfare has been paved.

But it is not modern pavement that has changed Main Street. Newspaper men and women from all over America beat a trail up Main Street to the mines. Yesterday I counted forty of them waiting for the official bulletin.

The townspeople and the visiting newspaper people no longer stop every man as he comes off shift to get

the latest prediction about the day of rescue. Everyone
has ceased to look for the gift of prophecy and has settled down to calm acceptance.

On the makeshift press platform, Ernestine, Ruth Finney, and
the other reporters were feeling the effects of too little sleep and
the intense late summer heat. With a cloudless sky and no
breeze, the metal roof of the old sawmill transformed the structure into a giant open-air broiler. The sour odor of hot sawdust
made the air thick, and sticky sap oozed from the rough pine
boards, clinging to everything it touched.

It had been a long ordeal for everyone involved. And even
with the end in sight, the ever-growing anticipation seemed to
induce more fatigue than excitement.

"The small army of press correspondents and cameramen
look like a small army, too," wrote a *San Francisco Call* reporter. "They are dressed in khaki, mostly, with flannel or out-
ing shirts, generally open at the collar. On all night shifts
sweaters or overcoats are affected. It is hot as the mischief here
in the daylight hours, but toward morning it gets rather chilly,
sitting under the little tin roofed shed with air walls."

Ruth had long since abandoned any concern for her appearance. Her hair stuck to her head in damp strands and a long
ribbon that was once neatly tied around her neck in a big bow
now hung loosely from the open collar of her blouse. She and
Tom Trebell took turns working at a crude desk and bench they
had constructed out of old crates. The press corps' designated
courier, Ed Doherty, of the *Chicago Tribune,* would occasionally stroll over from the mine office to give them some small
morsel of news that had made its way to the surface. Rescue
crews had searched the Argonaut 4200 level and found nothing
of interest. They were now exploring the 4350 drift.

5:30 P.M., Monday, September 18—Day 22

As the day wore on, reporters filed stories of both hopefulness and gloom. In an effort to bring some spark of optimism, several newspapers published early morning extras stating that the mine was found nearly free of gas. In their rush to get information, the reporters apparently didn't make the logical assumption that the clearing of the mine air was entirely due to increased ventilation from the newly opened connection with the Kennedy.

All of the reporters on the platform were settled in for the long haul. No one wanted to take the chance that the big break in the story would hit just at the moment they had driven into town for lunch. They sent their assistants for sandwiches and coffee or a chocolate bar to get them through the hungry hour. During slow times, they stretched out on one of the plank tables for a brief nap, only to be awakened by the rattling of telegraph keys as representatives of San Francisco newspapers performed their hourly check-in.

For more than twelve hours, the platform's single incoming phone line was in constant use as newspaper editors pressed their reporters for some tidbit of information that might not have already been published by their competitors. Late in the afternoon, after one of the reporters hung up the receiver, the phone immediately rang again. He put the earpiece back to his ear. "You've reached Hades—Satan speaking," he jokingly answered as the sweat ran down his face. After listening to the caller for a moment, he turned and scanned the platform. "Finney," he shouted. "Your turn."

Ruth Finney stood up from her improvised desk and walked over to the corner post of the platform where the telephone had been installed. With the deadline for the evening edition looming, *Sacramento Star* editor Harold Matson was hoping for a progress report. The *Star* planned to run the first installment of

Irving Moore's undercover story along with the latest update on the search for the miners. But for the first time in three weeks, Finney had nothing to report. In the past twenty-four hours, she had already given Matson enough copy to produce five extras.

"We're down to a waiting game," she told him. "I'll do my best to get word to you as soon as anything breaks."

Just as she started to hang up the receiver, she happened to glance toward the mine office and saw Ed Doherty running toward the platform at full stride.

"That's right," she quickly spoke into the receiver. "Something could break at any minute. We're just waiting. I'll get something right to you. You can expect something anytime now."

Matson was confused by her babbling for only a moment, then he turned to his assistant. "Stand by the teletype!" he shouted. "And tell the press room to get ready for another extra."

As the courier reached the platform, the reporters waited in dead silence. Breathlessly, Doherty told them that rescuers had located a bulkhead in a crosscut on the 4350 level of the mine and they were sure that the missing miners were there, but no sounds had been heard from behind the barricade.

"I shouted the news to Matson and he shouted it to our operator sentence by sentence," Finney recalled. "Most of the competition was too busy to watch, but my friend from the AP, Tom Trebell, stood beside me, looking on with a tortured face. He still had to write his bulletin and send it to Jackson by messenger—as I would have had to do if word had not come at the moment when I had an open line to my office."

Within the hour, the *Star*'s sixth extra had hit the streets with a bold (and somewhat assumptive) headline proclaiming "Bodies Are Located in Argonaut Mine."

At the fresh air station on the 4200 level of the Argonaut, Pickard was having trouble getting enough clean drinking water for the workers. The constricted and unstable condition of the

The front page of *Sacramento Star* extra #6, produced just minutes after reporter Ruth Finney's propitious phone call.

Kennedy 3600 raise made it difficult to bring anything larger than a small keg or canteen through the narrow passageway. Even the apparatus teams were having difficulty moving through the raise with their backpacks. One of the crew members received a severe gash in the forehead when he slipped while trying to work his way up the muddy incline.

Pickard assigned additional crews to enlarge the raise and install extra supporting timbers and ladder rungs so that men could move through safely and water barrels could be brought through into the Argonaut. Enlarging the raise would also facilitate the difficult process of removing survivors and/or bodies.

5:45 P.M., Monday, September 18—Day 22

Late Monday afternoon, apparatus team B2 created an opening in the compressed air pipe in the Argonaut 4350 crosscut, allowing fresh air to be blown in via the newly completed connection with the Kennedy pipe. The team members were then ordered to walk briskly in and out of the crosscut to facilitate the mixing of fresh air with bad air. Within minutes, the crosscut had been cleared of carbon monoxide up to the location of the first bulkhead. The crew then tested the air behind the second bulkhead by using a long pole to insert a canary cage through the unfinished section of the wall. When the cage was withdrawn, the bird lay lifeless on its floor.

It now seemed pointless to worry about forcing bad air in on possible survivors. Under the direction of First Aid Miner B. F. McDonald, team B2, wearing Gibbs apparatus, began dismantling the second barrier. Within a few minutes, there was an opening large enough for McDonald to crawl through. As his crew continued to pull down the wall, he climbed over the rubble and dropped down onto the other side. Just as he had expected, the flame of his carbide lamp was immediately snuffed out by the lack of oxygen. He adjusted his face mask so that it fit more tightly against his cheek and pulled a flashlight from his belt, directing its soft yellow beam into the dark passageway. As the light reflected off the wet floor, he noticed that there were many large puddles of water throughout the crosscut, some of them several inches deep.

Just a few feet beyond the second bulkhead, the crosscut branched off in three directions. McDonald could just make out the end of the main passageway straight ahead. Crew member Will Buckley joined him, and they moved forward toward the face of the crosscut. As they reached the intersection of the three forks, McDonald turned his light into the southerly branch. It was little more than a small room, not 10 feet wide in any direction. The floor was covered by several inches of water. Against one wall of the room sat what appeared to be a large dark bundle. The two men might have missed seeing it, if not for a covering of gray velvety fur that sparkled in the flashlight's beam. They moved closer and directed their lights on the

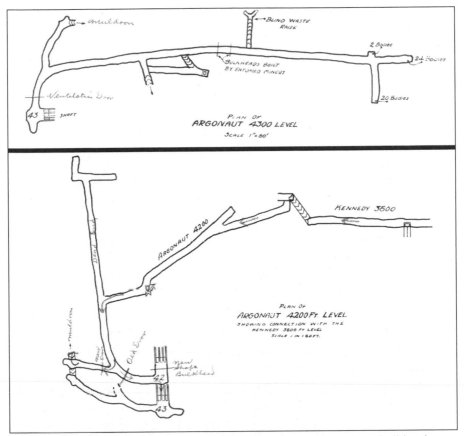

From the Bureau of Mines report, two maps show the location of two bulkheads built by the trapped miners.

damp, fuzzy mass. Buckley's eyes widened and he stumbled backward into the main room of the crosscut.

"I'm about out of air," he gasped excitedly. "I'm going back."

McDonald knew that it wasn't a lack of oxygen that sent his comrade running; it was the same terror and sickness that now tore at his own gut. Huddled together before him were the remains of two of the trapped Argonaut miners. Their nearly naked bodies were badly decomposed and covered in a thick layer of velvety mold, so the two men were now melded as one. They would later be identified as Charles and Arthur O'Berg, father and son. Overcome by nausea and emotion, McDonald crawled back to the other side of the bulkhead and ordered his team to return to the fresh air station.

At 7 P.M., rescue team B1 was sent to the surface and recovery team C1 was directed to the 4350 crosscut. This fresh air team consisted of both Argonaut and Kennedy miners who had been selected from crews that drove the Kennedy 3600 drift. The 36ers had just announced that each member of the team, by unanimous vote, would donate his share of the $5000 break-through reward to the widows and orphans of the forty-seven Argonaut miners.

As in their previous role, recovery team C1 remained under the direction of Argonaut foreman Doc Murphy and Kennedy foreman Bill Sinclair. This time, they would also be accompanied by Daniel Harrington and Orr Woodburn from the Bureau of Mines. Because many of the men on this team had previously worked with members of the ill-fated August 27 Argonaut late shift, Byron Pickard hoped they would be able to perform initial identification of bodies. Red Cross volunteers had prepared folds of cloth dipped in camphor, which team members held over their nose and mouth, hoping to camouflage the stench of the death chamber.

As they moved through the three branches of the crosscut, the sickening odor and the knowledge that this horrible display of decomposed flesh was once their comrades was overwhelming. (Ironically, the bulkheads that had failed to keep out the poisonous carbon monoxide had worked perfectly to seal in the gases formed by putrefaction, thus foiling Dr. Duschak's ongoing tests for those gases.) Members of the recovery team

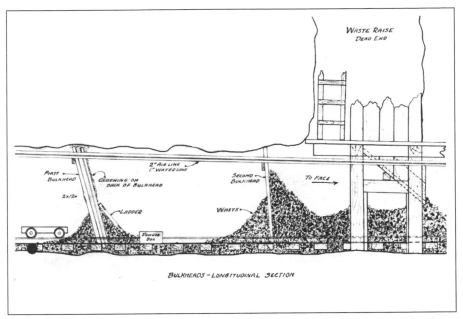

A detailed drawing from Byron Pickard's official report shows how two bulkheads were constructed by the entombed miners in the Argonaut 4350.

who were able to continue the body count refused to touch or move the corpses and could therefore identify only those men whose faces were visible.

Near the end of the crosscut, Woodburn made a startling discovery. At the base of a smooth greenstone slate wall lay the body of a miner with an outstretched hand holding a carbide lamp. Instinctively, Woodburn directed his light to the wall above the body. By pressing the flame of his lamp against the smooth face of the wall to create a black carbon residue, it appeared that this miner had documented the last hours of his existence. The first words were "3 o/clock gas getting strong"; then the time "3²⁰"; followed by "4 o'clock," with the "ock" trailing off as if the writer was unable to finish.

The body found at the base of the "message wall" was identified underground by several team members as Bill Fessel. The name *Fessel* was also written on the wall, and this was logically presumed to be the signature of the impromptu historian. In the days and weeks to come, miner Edward William Fessel would become more closely linked with the Argonaut Mine disaster than any other person.

While the recovery team was working to identify bodies, Byron Pickard visited the crosscut in order to get a firsthand idea of the conditions. He quickly realized that fresh air teams could not safely continue to work there. Several of the men had already passed out from the effects of residual carbon monoxide and the unbearable odor of rotting flesh.

Before they were recalled, members of team C1 were able to make an initial count of forty-two bodies scattered throughout the three branches of the crosscut. They were certain that most, if not all, of the forty-seven men would be found there, but an accurate count was impossible because of the condition of the bodies and the fact that many of them were huddled or piled together.

On Pickard's orders, the rest of the work would be performed by apparatus men. He was now fully aware that recovery of the bodies would be no easy matter. Because of the advanced state of decay, the remains were extremely fragile. He sent Harrington to the surface with instructions to request the assistance of experts in the recovery of badly decomposed corpses.

8 P.M., Monday, September 18—Day 22

Mary Warrington arrived at the Kennedy office as Fred Lowell finished writing his latest bulletin. For three weeks, she had anticipated and dreaded the conversation that was about to take place.

"I'm sure you're already prepared for this," Lowell said quietly as he handed her a copy of the notice. "But I wanted to give you time to make the necessary notifications before I give it to the press."

Even before she read the first word, tears welled in her eyes.

September 18, 1922, Bulletin No. 49

7:45 P.M.—Mr. McDonald and his mine rescue crew just came to the surface and reported that they were inside the second bulkhead where they found thirty bodies. It was impossible to complete the count of the bodies. From the appearance of the bodies, the men appear to have been dead for at least several days.

7:55 P.M.—Mr. Pickard has been inside the second temporary bulkhead on the 4350 level, Argonaut, and counted forty-two bodies. He is quite positive that there are more at that point.

A single tear escaped and was quickly wiped from her cheek with the stroke of an index finger. "Can you give me about thirty minutes?" she asked Lowell.

"I don't think that will be a problem," he answered. "But you know how fast word spreads among the miners. You'll need to move quickly."

"I understand." She quickly regained her composure. "And thank you for your thoughtfulness."

Minutes later, having gathered her tireless little army of nurses in the shadows outside the Red Cross canteen, Warrington quietly relayed the dreaded news. During the past twenty-two days, each of the twenty Red Cross women had been assigned to care for one or more families. Now they would be called upon to bring the worst possible news to those mothers, wives, and children. Optimism had been unrewarded. There was no miracle. There were no survivors.

"Out to those little homes that dot the smooth rolling slopes beyond Jackson village they sped," wrote a reporter for the *San Francisco Examiner,* "the women of the Red Cross, bearers of the dread Fate that all Jackson has feared but would not allow itself to put into words. And they passed through main street—wrapped in a tenseness beyond any it has evero known in all its strange and varied history of the fevered hunt for gold. . . . The strength of brother love that has filled the pages of poetry and prose throughout the ages was written in an imperishable flesh and blood record in this tragedy of the California hills."

Warrington herself would accompany those nurses who had been assigned to notify the pregnant wives. She wanted to assure that the unborn children of the Argonaut victims were given the best possible chance to survive the emotional devastation soon to be inflicted upon their mothers. Surprisingly, after all the notifications were made, only one woman required medical attention: Emily Ludekins, alleged mistress of miner Charles Fitzgerald, attempted to commit suicide by drinking Lysol cleaning fluid.

"The fortitude shown by these women is truly wonderful," Warrington said of the miners' wives. "The terrible suspense of twenty-one days during which they were one day buoyed up with hope and the next plunged into the fear almost too much, it would seem, to be borne. . . . They are bearing up in splendid fashion. I guess it is because they are like the women who have lived near battlefields. They have accepted the inevitable with a fine resignation."

Warrington had also been asked by the executive committee to petition the miners' families to agree to three mass funerals—Catholic, Protestant, and Greek Orthodox—each to be held one hour apart. Prior to the breakthrough, many of the families had expressed their desire for a single mass burial with no ceremonies, but they now yielded to Warrington's tender appeal.

Members of the Salvation Army and other community
volunteers arrive at the Argonaut Mine with food for
rescue workers and the miners' families.

As Warrington and her nurses comforted stricken families,
the news that all of the miners had been found dead reached the
streets of Jackson. A small group of citizens gathered around a
telephone pole at the Court Street corner that had become the
town's unofficial bulletin board. "Dead," one of the men whis-
pered in disbelief as he read the latest posting. "All dead."

As word moved through the town, other groups of citizens
gathered on sidewalks and hotel steps, talking quietly for a few

moments before going on their way. Soon, the doors of businesses were shut, and buzzing neon signs fell silent.

"Jackson took what it heard with sober stoicism," the *Chronicle* would declare.

"Grief has struck too trenchant for words," proclaimed the *Call*. "Fate has dealt too cruelly for whimper."

Several of the miners' families had already left town; others were preparing to move in with relatives in other cities. The throng of volunteer miners who had tarried for twenty-two days with hopes of participating in the rescue now headed back to their old jobs or moved on in search of new work. Some, having learned a somber lesson, would never again toil beneath the earth's surface.

10 P.M., Monday, September 18—Day 22

Throughout the evening, crews worked to install additional air hoses into the end of the 4350 crosscut in order to improve air quality. They also began construction of a hoisting system that would facilitate bringing the bodies from the 4350 to the 4200 station. On the surface, carpenters prepared a number of make-shift gurneys to be used in conjunction with the temporary hoist. These gurneys would make the 150-foot trip on the same rails that had guided the Argonaut skip. The rails would be heavily greased to reduce friction. The milk and resuscitation supplies that had been brought to the 4200 fresh air station were sent back to the surface, soon to be replaced by rubber gloves, deodorizing powders, rolls of heavy canvas, and stacks of black rubber body bags.

Although the executive committee had always kept up the outward appearance of optimism, they had been preparing for the worst as early as the second week of the disaster. Under the

During a break in rescue efforts, crew members read newspaper accounts of the long-awaited breakthrough into the Argonaut 4200 crosscut.

committee's direction, undertakers Ralph McGee and S. E. Woodworth had laid out a detailed recovery plan that included various casket companies, the State Board of Health, the State Compensation Insurance Fund, the Amador County coroner's office, and a team of fifteen volunteer undertakers supervised by the secretary of the State Board of Embalmers, Bessie Gustason.

Forty-seven caskets previously ordered from a San Francisco supplier had been placed in storage at the Martell rail terminal. Byron Pickard now instructed McGee to have these caskets

Sacramento Star reporter Ruth Finney, looking disheveled but triumphant after scooping the competition.

brought to the Argonaut mill, where Gustason was organizing a temporary morgue and preparing to receive bodies.

Shortly after midnight, all of the recovery crews were sent home with orders to get a good night's sleep in anticipation of what was sure to be a long and arduous recovery process. The bodies of the forty-seven Argonaut miners would remain in their temporary tomb for one more night. A sentry at the 4200 station would guard the door.

Midnight, Monday, September 18—Day 22

After standing in line at the telephone company office for nearly an hour, Ruth Finney held the receiver to her ear and prepared to file her final story of the day. Even though the *Daily News* had sent her two assistants, Ruth still preferred to make at least some of the calls herself, especially to the *Star*. Once again she heard the operator's familiar rapid exordium, "Main 6200 Sacramento? Collect from Miss Finney?" During the past fifteen hours, the *Star* had printed ten extra editions, all of them with 2-inch headlines and bold Ruth Finney bylines.

During the past day and a half, Ruth had slept a total of four hours, eaten one stale doughnut, and drank more cups of coffee than she could count. She was dirty, hungry, and sleepy, but she had scored the scoop of a lifetime, and her stories were running in hundreds of newspapers nationwide. She had just one final detail to take care of. Her advance story, written with the help of the gun shop Bible, could now be published.

"And Matson," she added as she wrapped up her report, "don't forget to run the resurrection story."

"It's already typeset," he replied. "And it went out on the wire two hours ago."

CHAPTER 11

They Have Risen

8 A.M., Tuesday, September 19—Day 23

Recovery of the remains of the Argonaut miners began on the morning of September 19 with a careful count to assure that all forty-seven men had been located. Twenty-four bodies were found at the end of the main branch of the crosscut, twenty-one in the north branch, and two in the south branch, for a confirmed total of forty-seven. Having every reason to believe the count was correct, Fred Lowell communicated this information to the press in his final official release:

10:10 A.M., September 19, 1922, Bulletin No. 50

Mr. Pickard, U.S. Bureau of Mines, telephoned word to Mr. Bullard from underground stating that an official count of the bodies had been made and that a total of forty-seven had been found in the 4350 level crosscut. This being the number of men underground according to official records, it now remains for the rescue crews both in oxygen breathing apparatus and without to bring these bodies to the surface as soon as possible.

Now designated as a recovery crew, apparatus team A1 would begin the challenging and morbid task of removing the miners' remains. They would be assisted by a group of consulting undertakers who had been called in by the Bureau of Mines on the recommendation of Bessie Gustason.

In typical forensic practice related to multiple-victim catastrophes, even the most deteriorated corpses are usually found fully or partially clothed. This clothing helps to keep tissue in place and facilitates moving the remains to a morgue or funerary establishment, where the clothing can then be carefully removed. In the case of the Argonaut miners, nearly all of their clothing had been used to chink the cracks in the makeshift bulkhead. Many of the miners then huddled together in their last minutes and remained that way after death, skin against skin. The dark, damp conditions of the crosscut hastened decomposition, and the flesh of life quickly became a disintegrating mass of mucilaginous tissue.

Whether in contact with other human flesh or the slate walls and floor of the crosscut, each body would have to be carefully pried loose, taking care to retain as much of the original structure as possible. These remains would then be wrapped in canvas held closed by safety pins and placed in a rubber body bag. This bag would be attached to a Stokes Navy stretcher and carried out to the 4350 station. There, the stretcher would be tied to one of the specially constructed wooden gurneys and hauled up to the Argonaut 4200 level. Two fresh air men would then carry the stretcher down the connecting raise and out through the Kennedy 3600 drift to the main shaft. Finally, each body would be individually brought to the surface in a Kennedy skip.

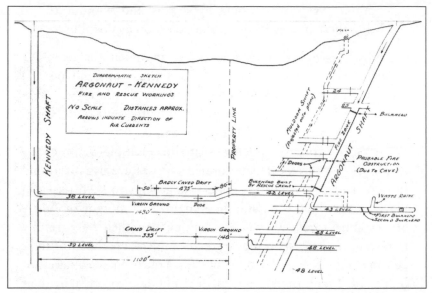

A simplified cross-section map shows the pertinent features of the Kennedy and Argonaut mines as they related to the rescue effort and discovery of bulkheads in the Argonaut 4350 drift.

It took more than two hours for the first body to be prepared and strapped in for the long journey to the Kennedy 3600 station. The stretcher was carefully placed on its end in the Kennedy skip, and the skip tender signaled the hoist house. At the surface, a throng of volunteers, Bureau of Mines personnel, reporters, and onlookers stood silently, waiting for the dreaded miner's dirge—three sets of three bells—the signal to hoist the body of a deceased comrade.

At 12:12 P.M. on September 19, twenty-two and one-half days after the discovery of the Argonaut fire, the remains of one of the forty-seven members of the Argonaut night shift returned to the surface. According to recovery workers, this was the body found at the base of the last-message wall, identified underground as that of Edward William Fessel.

* * *

Ruth Finney's resurrection story appeared on Tuesday in the *Sacramento Star* and in nearly every major West Coast newspaper. In the days that followed, it would be picked up by other newspapers across the United States. Written in an unusual semi-elegiac style and overflowing with religious sentimentalism, it tore at the heartstrings of a distraught nation:

MEN ARE NOT THERE, BUT THEY HAVE RISEN
by Ruth Finney

At the Argonaut Mine, Jackson, Calif., Sept. 19—Now upon the first day of the week, very early in the morning, they came up the sepulchre.

And they found the stone rolled away from the sepulchre.

And they entered in and found not the body of Lord Jesus.

And it came to pass—behold, two men stood by them in shining garments—and they said to them:

"He is not here, but is risen."

Very early in the morning, women of Jackson came to the shaft of the Kennedy mine where their men were buried.

And they found the stone cleared away from the shaft.

And they waited while men entered the shaft but found not their husbands and their brothers.

And as they stood in grief and despair, the women—some of them—heard again that message—

"They are not here, but are risen."

The long battle was a losing one. The fight was in vain.

No living man was found in the shaft of the Argonaut mine when the rescue crews broke through.

The bodies were there—but that was all.

"I am the resurrection and the life; he that believeth in Me, though he were dead, yet shall he live."

Defeat for the men and women on the surface.

Victory for the men, who, though they were dead, yet shall live.

For those men, no agonizing days and nights of blackness, buried alive in the mine shaft, helpless and waiting for help.

No endless hours of despair, of madness.

No battle with hunger, thirst, foul disease.

For through the long days of waiting, they were not there.

Bodies only, that felt not. Insensible flesh, dust returning to dust.

No escape for the bodies.

For the men there was escape. There was a way out.

"I am the way, the Truth, and the Life."

"In my Father's house are many mansions—Where I am there ye may be also."

Comfort, divine comfort, for the women who weep!

The real truth in Ruth Finney's story was that family and friends were honestly comforted by the knowledge that the miners had not suffered. During the first few days after the bodies were discovered, everyone praised the "historian" who documented the miners' last hours by burning a series of times onto the rock wall with the flame of his carbide lamp.

"William Fessel's note has comforted broken hearts in every home today," wrote a United Press reporter. "It proves that the men died only three hours after they were trapped. It takes away forever the thoughts of horror they feared the men suffered, and these were the hardest of all the hard things to bear."

Relying on "eyewitness" accounts from a variety of sources, not one newspaper accurately reported the true text of the "last message" in the first days following the breakthrough. Some embellished the scant information they had received. Others, having only a general idea of what had been written, simply invented their own versions. One newspaper reported that the message was burned into a board; several said it was scratched on a piece of paper and pinned to one of the miner's shirts.

The *San Francisco Examiner* and other newspapers described the writings as a full-fledged missive written on paper and pinned to one of the miner's jumpers: "3 A.M. Gas bad. Getting too strong. We are going to leave you. William Fessel." The "we are going to leave you" quote appeared in other newspapers as well, although no such note was ever reported by officials and the purported additional text does not appear in a later photograph of the wall. The *Sacramento Union,* having run an Associated Press version of the errant quote, later admitted the error and printed a correction.

Newspapers also erroneously reported that the bodies of the miners were lined up in perfect rows. The *Examiner* even provided a drawing of the "death chamber" that showed the bodies lying side by side in a perfectly spaced human chain. Although more than a few reporters wrote that the men were completely naked, official reports said that, although they did use much of their clothing in an attempt to seal the bulkhead, all of the miners had retained underwear and/or other garments. Some newspapers also mentioned evidence of a third attempted bulkhead, but this was later explained as simply piles of rock that were typically found in abandoned crosscuts. Perhaps most absurd among the fallacious reporting was a claim that all of the miners' watches had stopped at exactly the same time.

The removal of the miners' bodies was conducted in a very businesslike manner. No family members were present, having long since returned to their homes or the homes of family or friends. Mine workers who were not part of the recovery procedure had gone home as well. Members of the press kept their agreement; they watched from a distance. No photographs of the recovery process would appear in any newspaper.

As each body came to the surface, it was loaded into a waiting hearse and transported to the Argonaut mill, which sat atop the hill above the Argonaut Mine and overlooked both mines as well as the town of Jackson. Being the largest open building on the Argonaut property, the mill had been easily converted into a makeshift morgue and mortuary. The numerous long conveyor belts that three weeks earlier carried gold ore to the crushers now served perfectly as coffin biers.

An accurate official identification of the victims was the most crucial part of the recovery process. Bessie Gustason and her team of morticians cautiously extracted the remains from the body bags and placed them on an examination table. Clothing was removed and searched for brass checks or other identification. Embalming procedures were immediately undertaken to arrest decomposition, and chemicals were applied to eliminate as much of the odor as possible. Once the examination and identification process was complete, each body was wrapped in white linen and placed in a coffin. A sheet of paper bearing the miner's name and number was taped to the coffin lid.

5:00 P.M., Tuesday, September 19—Day 23

By 5 P.M., nine bodies had been brought out of the Argonaut 4350 crosscut. Realizing that the recovery teams were exhausted from the day's grueling and gruesome work, Pickard ordered everyone to the surface. For only the second time in three weeks,

The temporary mortuary at the Argonaut mill.

the crews would be able to sit down to a proper dinner and sleep in their own beds.

By nightfall, the grounds of the Kennedy and Argonaut properties were strangely quiet. And, for the first time in three weeks, Main Street in Jackson again bustled with nighttime activity as both miners and reporters shared an opportunity to drown their sorrows. But for some members of the recovery crew, there was not enough gin in all the speakeasies in California to erase the ghastly awfulness of this day.

Throughout the first day of the recovery process, Byron Pickard gathered information from the undertakers and recovery crews in an attempt to determine the movements of the men on the night of the fire. The number of lunch buckets found in the

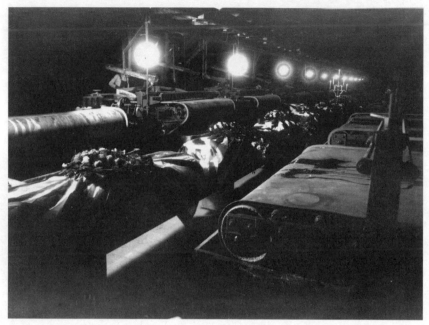

Rows of caskets containing the bodies of forty-six miners sit on conveyor belts in the Argonaut mill.

4500 station suggested that the men had gathered there to discuss a plan of action. The 4500 ventilation door was found open, indicating that the men had first attempted to make their way out through the ventilation raises leading to the Muldoon shaft. By the time they reached the 4350 level, they had probably realized that the smoke and fumes would overtake them long before they made it to the second exit, so they moved back into the 4350 drift, then into the long crosscut.

Pickard wondered why they did not leave the ventilation door in the 4350 drift open so that the smoke and gases would be drawn through the drift, rather than being allowed to accumulate and back up into the crosscut. He also found it curious that none of the men had attempted to go to levels above the 4350 and open the ventilation doors, which would have short-circuited the ventilation system and reduced the smoke and gas being pushed down upon them.

It was apparent that, as the miners moved through the 4350 drift, they had collected discarded dynamite boxes and other loose wood for use in building the bulkhead. At one point in the crosscut several months earlier, a raise had been driven to exploit an ore pocket above that level, and when work in the raise was abandoned, a large pile of waste rock had been left behind. The miners used this rock to construct their bulkhead.

"It is quite evident that before they completed their first bulkhead, gas was leaking through in sufficient quantities to cause distress," Pickard wrote in his report. "Otherwise they would not have taken the time and energy to build a second bulkhead twenty-five feet back of the first one. The second bulkhead was poorly built, indicating haste and weakness. . . . No excreta signs were found, there were no signs whatever to indicate struggles, impatience, or fear. . . . It is believed too, that at the time they completed their bulkhead there was con- siderable gas in the crosscut . . . [and that] the men died a few hours after the fire started."

8 A.M., Wednesday, September 20—Day 24

On Wednesday morning, a number of additional undertakers volunteered to go below and help the recovery crews, which greatly sped up the process. Deodorizing powders were applied throughout the end of the crosscut and fans were installed to help circulate fresh air, but recovery crews continued to wear Gibbs apparatus so that they could work comfortably in the malodorous atmosphere. Throughout the day, bodies arrived at the surface approximately every thirty minutes. During the overnight respite, various committees and their directors had taken the opportunity to fine-tune their operations, and all ele- ments of the recovery process now seemed glitch-free.

Despite having used much of their clothing in an attempt to seal the bulkhead, thirty-eight of the forty-seven Argonaut miners managed to retain their brass checks somewhere on their person. These thirty-eight were identified by the corresponding number on the Argonaut employment rolls. Brass check #83, belonging to Ernie Miller, was found in a pair of trousers that had been stuffed between the rocks of the bulkhead. Miller's body was later identified by his father-in-law and by the wedding band he still wore. Identifying disc #109 was found on the floor of the crosscut. The body of the miner who would have carried that number, Marko Janovich, would later be identified by his good friend Niko Quirolo, who operated the concentrator machine in the Argonaut mill.

The bodies of six other Argonaut victims carrying no brass check and having no familiar identifying characteristics were identified by officials of the mine, coworkers, or close relatives—or, in some cases, a combination of these. Strangely, the brass identification discs that some of the miners carried into the mine were never located.

The miner whose body had been found lying at the base of the last-message wall, and who had been identified underground as William Fessel, had retained his brass check in his pocket. This check, however, was not Fessel's #122. Accordingly, this body was not identified as William Fessel, but as the miner whose name appeared on the Argonaut rolls next to the number found on the identifying disc. (Adding to the mystery, the disc number and associated name were never divulged by officials.)

At 8:30 P.M., Pickard received word from crews in the 4350 crosscut that only four bodies remained to be recovered.

He quickly checked his tally sheet. Four more bodies would bring the total to forty-six.

He called to the surface for a recount of the bodies that had already been sent up. There was no question among the surface workers—so far, forty-two bodies had been brought up.

On Pickard's orders, recovery crews again carefully searched every inch of the 4350 crosscut. They reported back that there were exactly four bodies remaining to be brought out.

Once all the recovered bodies had reached the surface, Pickard ordered a thorough exploration of the entire 4350 level of the Argonaut Mine. Crews searched every stope and raise. They looked in every hole and under every pile of rock. They found no evidence of a forty-seventh miner. Several of the team members started down the manway ladder with the intention of exploring below the 4350 level, but they found that the mine was filled with water to a point approximately 100 feet above the 4500 station. If a forty-seventh body was going to be found, it would have to be above the 4350 level of the mine—or in the flooded lower levels.

9:30 P.M., Wednesday, September 20—Day 24

In the makeshift morgue at the Argonaut mill, as undertakers prepared the last body for placement in a casket, Bessie Gustason pulled brass check #204 from the pocket of a damp and moldy denim jumper. She picked up her copy of the Argonaut employee roster and checked off the name of Evan Ely, then carefully looked over the pages to assure that everything was in order. During the past two days, she had checked off forty-six numbers. Only miner #122 remained unaccounted for.

Earlier that evening, the putrefied clothing taken from the miners' bodies was carried to the edge of the Argonaut property, doused with kerosene, and burned. When the employee assigned to the grim duty returned to make sure the material had been completely consumed, he noticed a golden glint in the smoldering ashes. He fished out an ordinary signet ring with the initials JSN and turned it over to Bessie Gustason. She scanned her list of the forty-seven miners. The initials matched none of the names.

At the Argonaut change house, the miners' street clothing was collected and identified so that it could be returned to surviving family members. With the help of the Argonaut foreman, Red Cross volunteers carefully identified forty-seven sets of clothing and placed them in boxes, each marked with the owner's name. As the foreman made one final check of the change house, he found another set of street clothes hanging from a hook. He and the Red Cross nurses double-checked the boxes. All forty-seven were accounted for. The forty-eighth set of clothing contained no identification and was never claimed.

At 10 P.M., a physically drained and mentally frustrated Byron Pickard decided to call it a day. The remaining search crews were ordered to the surface and a new official count was given to the press. The only explanation that he could provide was that the original count—a count performed by four separate individuals, all of whom arrived at the same total—was incorrect. Later that evening, sitting up in bed in his hotel room, he scanned the names and numbers on Gustason's list for what must have been the hundredth time. The mistake made in counting the bodies was bad enough, but why did it have to be the body of *this* miner that was unaccounted for? The question would occupy his mind through a long and sleepless night.

Under the stark lighting of the Argonaut mill, forty-seven flag-draped coffins sat on a series of conveyer belts that once carried gold ore to the thundering crushers.

One coffin remained empty.

One miner, Edward William Fessel—the man whose name was boldly written on the last-message wall, the man who newspapers had called the "historian" of the Argonaut tragedy—was now officially listed as missing.

CHAPTER 12

Bound for
the Same Place

4 A.M., Thursday, September 21—Day 25

In the early morning hours of September 21, a series of explosions rocked Jackson, shaking many of the town's residents from their sleep. It took only a few minutes for most of the community to realize that these blasts did not come from the mines. The resonance was sadly familiar.

During the first two decades of the twentieth century, the ravages of a world war, a devastating influenza epidemic, and the perils of a flourishing and ever-changing mining industry helped swell Jackson's three little cemeteries far beyond the size originally intended by the town's gold rush residents. Once separated by several hundred feet of open space, the Catholic, Protestant, and Greek Orthodox cemeteries had merged by 1922 into a blanket of headstones and crosses that covered three rolling hills above North Main Street.

Once all of the hilltop plots were occupied, grave diggers began to move down the slopes where erosion had exposed the familiar greenstone shale and quartz that lined the drifts and stopes of the mines. Here, ironically, on three separate hillsides just a few hundred feet apart, the graves of forty-seven miners were being dug with the basic tools of mining—picks and shovels, drills and dynamite. Because this unusually large number of graves had to be excavated as quickly as possible, the work was performed entirely by miners from the Argonaut.

The cost of the miners' interment, approximately $175 per body, would be borne by the Argonaut Mining Company and the California State Compensation Insurance Fund. Arrangements were coordinated by the management of the Argonaut Mine in cooperation with the Amador County chapter of the Red Cross.

Throughout the day, friends and loved ones passed by the forty-seven flag-draped caskets at the Argonaut mill. One casket still remained empty, but at the time nearly everyone believed that the body of missing miner William Fessel would be found somewhere in the mine. Forty-seven graves had been dug, and Reverend William Brown of the Methodist Episcopal Church planned to include Fessel's name in graveside services at the Protestant cemetery.

In the depths of the Argonaut, search teams continued to look for the remains of the forty-seventh miner. The mine's sump pump had not operated since the fire burned through electric wires on the first day of the disaster. Water from firefighting efforts, combined with the usual daily seepage from shafts and drifts, now filled the working levels of the mine below 4400 feet. The search was therefore confined to the 4200 and 4350 levels of the Argonaut, with particular concentration on stopes and connecting raises, including those leading to the Muldoon shaft.

In his room at the National Hotel, freelance reporter and photographer Aird MacDonald prepared for two very important assignments. First, he had been chosen by the Bureau of Mines to photographically document the areas of the Argonaut where rescue and recovery efforts took place. He would be the only photographer permitted to take pictures underground.

The next day, MacDonald would have an equally important but far less adventurous duty to carry out. As an elder of the Mormon Church, he would be called upon to bless the grave of Evan Ely, the only victim of the disaster practicing the Mormon faith, whose body would be interred with his comrades in the Protestant cemetery.

Primed for his own personal photo op, Aird MacDonald arrived at the Argonaut on Thursday morning dressed in a crisp new miner's uniform: a pair of denim work pants with the cuffs rolled up and a four-pocket denim jumper. With his camera slung over his shoulder and carrying a heavy wooden tripod, he donned a miner's hat and a carbide lamp and crawled into a skip with Bureau of Mines representatives Daniel Harrington and B. F. McDonald. His description of the adventure published in the *Sacramento Star* is written in a style suspiciously similar to that of *Star* city editor Ruth Finney:

A flash of a descent of 3600 feet in the skip, a low ceilinged chamber in the bowels of the earth, a climb on hands and knees in the muck up the raise and—

The place where these men died. Six feet high. Five feet wide. Black, sinister walls of mud and rock, seeping with water. . . .

My throat was dry and parched from the gas. My lungs heavy.

The gloom was deep. The carbide lights on our miners' caps cast weird shadows around the death chamber and sketched uncanny shapes on the wall, silent witness to the death struggle of brave men.

The death pit was in the shape of a cross. . . . At the far end of the main tunnel, my guides, miners, focused

Accompanying photographer Aird MacDonald into the Argonaut Mine, Bureau of Mines officials examine the remains of the first bulkhead in the Argonaut 4350 crosscut.

their lights on the wall. . . . I saw before me the message from the dead.

It was sketched by Wm. Fessel with his carbide light in a bold, scrawny hand; burned into the rock by the light of a man who knew death was near.

Using flashbulb lighting, MacDonald photographed the last-message wall, the entrance to the 4350 crosscut, the remains of the two bulkheads, and each end of the Kennedy–Argonaut connecting raise. He also took a portrait of rescue crew A1 seated in the Argonaut 4200 fresh air station as they took a break from their continuing search for the missing forty-seventh miner.

Officials examine the remains of the second bulkhead.

When MacDonald's photograph of the message wall was printed, it revealed additional writing that could only have been seen in bright light. Using the sharp edge of a rock, one of the trapped miners had scratched into the slate, "3:15—half knocked out."

MacDonald's photograph provided a clear document of the miners' last hours. First, miner #1, using his carbide lamp, wrote "3 o/clock, gas getting strong, Fessel." Then miner #2 scratched "3:15, half knocked out." Miner #1 wrote "3²⁰." Miner #2 scratched "3³⁵" in the F of miner #1's "Fessel." Finally, miner #1 wrote "4 o/cl." This was the final entry.

Because no dates or days of the week were written, the inscriptions seemed to clearly indicate that just three and one-half hours after the fire was discovered, the miners had finished barricading themselves in the end of the Argonaut 4350 crosscut and were being overcome by carbon monoxide. By 3:15 A.M.

Aird MacDonald's photograph of the message wall showed details that had previously gone unnoticed.

on Monday morning, half of the men were unconscious. Since the last notation was written at 4 A.M., it was highly probable that all of the miners were unconscious by 4:15 and that all had perished by sunrise Monday morning.

While the notations left by the two miners provided a general timeline of their last hours, it also presented a paradox. Once the two bulkheads built by the trapped miners were in place, there was no way to escape. If miner #1 was William Fessel, why was his body not found in the crosscut? If he was not William Fessel, why did miner #1 sign or write the name Fessel at the end of his message?

Some Bureau of Mines personnel believed that miner #1 was trying to say that Fessel was not among the men behind the barricade but that he was unable to complete the message because he was overcome by fumes. Others pointed out that miner #1 was still writing times on the wall an hour later—it would have been easy for him to add "not here" or "gone for help" below Fessel's name. Since the bulkhead was surely in place before the times and other notations were written, it would not have been possible for Fessel to write them, then exit the sealed-off crosscut. Logically, whoever wrote the messages would have perished with his comrades behind the barricade.

By nightfall on Thursday, September 21, searchers had found no sign of the missing forty-seventh miner. When a new team of volunteers arrived at the 4200 fresh air station, Byron Pickard suggested they call it a day and begin their exploration again after the funerals. The men asked if they could continue the search into the night—they hoped to locate Fessel's body so that he could be buried with his comrades. Pickard was now sure that a forty-seventh body would not be found in the accessible portions of the mine, but he understood why the men wanted to keep trying.

In the predawn hours of September 22, as a procession of trucks carried the coffins from the Argonaut mill and distributed them among Jackson's three cemeteries, yet another tired and disappointed search team made its way back through the Argonaut–Kennedy connection and up to the surface. Forty-seven coffins would be interred. One would remain empty.

6 A.M., Friday, September 22—Day 26

As Ruth Finney pulled her new gray cloche hat down over her short red tresses, she looked out the window of her hotel room and watched the morning twilight give way to bright sunlight that cast jagged shadows along Jackson's newly paved Main Street. After lying awake for most of the night, she finally decided to get out of bed and take her time preparing for the eventful day ahead.

The first funeral, an open-air requiem mass for twenty-two Catholic miners, wasn't scheduled to start until 9 A.M., but Ruth could already see small groups of well-dressed citizens walking somberly toward the north end of town. These were surely mourners, since all of Jackson's schools and businesses had been ordered closed by the town's board of trustees.

Ruth walked down the stairs to the lobby and glanced around, hoping to find a familiar face. Her friend Tom Trebell and several of the other reporters had gone home, and most of those who stayed to cover the funerals were still catching up on hours of lost sleep. She decided to go ahead on her own.

As she strolled up Main Street, it suddenly struck her that she had never really taken in her surroundings. She had walked this street many times in the past three weeks, but for twenty-two days her entire thought process was concentrated on the story—the mine, the miners, their families. Now she read the names of the businesses and wondered: Can this town ever be the same? How can they possibly recover from such tragedy?

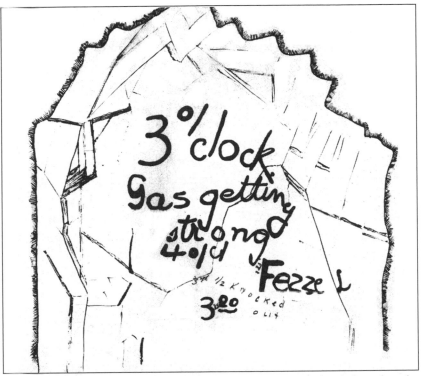

The Bureau of Mines recreated the miners' last messages in sketch form based on the original photograph by Aird MacDonald.

The street leading up to the Catholic cemetery was steep, and Ruth was out of breath when she slipped past the narrow iron gate with the ever-increasing throng of mourners. A large crowd had already gathered at the grave sites, and she made her way around the edge so that she could get a clear, if distant, view of the ceremony. The effect of a long, rainless summer was evident in the crunch of brown grass and swirls of fine dust produced by the mass of trampling feet. An abundant display of flowers and decorations prepared by students from Jackson High School surrounded the graves and provided a welcome bit of color in the drab landscape. With sweat pouring down their cheeks, the uniformed Jackson City Band played a mournful dirge.

Reporters had been given advance copies of the text for the Catholic and Protestant services, and Ruth glanced down at the names of the Argonaut miners who would be laid to rest in this, the first of three ceremonies. Most of the names, many of them Italian, were now familiar to her. Several stood out: George Steinman, who expressed foreboding that Sunday night, and whose wife had opened her home to Ruth and her *Sacramento Star* photographer; Emanuel Olobardi, who also had a premonition of danger; Charles Fitzgerald, whose presumed mistress attempted suicide upon learning of his death; Pio Oliva, whose brother would have met the same fate, if not for a propitious decision to take the weekend off; and the Leon brothers, whose family members would soon arrive in Jackson unaware of the sad news that awaited them.

By 9 A.M., when Father Michael O'Connell began speaking, over one thousand people filled the wide expanse of cemetery around the long row of twenty-seven graves. Mary Warrington and her Red Cross nurses, dressed in bright white uniforms and coif, stood out boldly against the sea of gray and black. The priest's words wafted in and out on a hot September breeze as Ruth attempted to follow along with her advance text. At one point, she almost felt as if he were scolding her for her resurrection story, and she wondered if she had made the right decision in publishing such an emotional piece so soon after the tragedy.

"God forbid that at a moment such as this that I should use mere words to play on your emotions or to stir your hearts to great depths of sympathy at this side of death," Father O'Connell proclaimed. "I therefore will not dwell on the details of the tragedy. We here in Jackson knew these men; they were our neighbors and comrades. We know of their daily labor and sacrifice for families and friends and we know that when the

Rescue and recovery team A1 photographed by Aird MacDonald in the Argonaut 4200 station.

supreme moment came they were not found wanting in faith and courage. They did not surrender to fear or flee in panic. They died like the men they were, fighting to the very last."

Ruth was surprised at how quiet the large crowd seemed. Even the children, many of whom could not have understood why they were there, seemed to stand silently by their parents—inquisitive yet undemanding. As Father O'Connell's last words echoed through the stillness, the bell in the tower of the Catholic church began to peal, triggering a cry of grief from one of the miners' wives. Other cries followed, and once again Mary Warrington's nurses moved forward to comfort the stricken. Italy's consul general, Vincente Fileti, then closed the ceremony with words of consolation to the community.

The two remaining ceremonies were carefully scheduled to allow time for people to move from one location to the next. As she cautiously negotiated a sea of headstones and the still growing throng of mourners, Ruth Finney scanned the crowd for notables. All three members of the executive committee were in attendance, as were familiar faces from the Bureau of Mines and the Industrial Accident Commission. She also noticed that Governor Stephens, who was in San Francisco on state business, had sent his personal secretary, Arthur Keech, to represent him at the funerals.

By the time the crowd had settled into position around the next group of miners' graves, the morning heat had become oppressive. The audience searched for anything they could use to stir the air, and the assemblage rippled with determined fanning. Like Father O'Connell, Reverend William Brown of Jackson's Methodist Episcopal church took great care to avoid placing blame for the deaths of the nine men being interred in the Protestant cemetery.

"This is not the time nor place to discuss the phases of the disaster which bear upon the continual safety of the men working underground," he declared. "That will be done by those technically competent with the matter. But it is very fitting that we should on this occasion give emphasis to the value put upon human life, and extol those noble qualities that have been so conspicuous in the work of rescue. Never can we say that life is held cheaply when we have such a demonstration as this."

As Reverend Brown read the names of the nine miners, Ruth Finney was again reminded of the stories connected with some of them: Elmer Bacheller, who was not a regular Argonaut employee and was working that night as a favor for a friend; the O'Bergs, father and son, who worked together for the first and last time that night; Bert Seamans, whose own father learned that his long-lost son was among the trapped miners when he read newspaper accounts of the disaster; and,

Site of the miners' graves in Jackson's Catholic cemetery.

of course, Ernest Miller, who was lucky enough to survive being trapped by a mine fire once but not twice.

One of the miners interred in the Protestant cemetery was in fact Catholic. Charles Fitzgerald would be laid to rest beside his Protestant chum, James Clayton, at the request of both families. "Religion does not matter," Charles's brother Sam told members of the press. "They are both bound for the same place." Clayton's fiancée, Myrtle Richards, whose first husband was killed in a mining accident, would find this ceremony particularly agonizing.

"We are glad to think they met death bravely," Reverend Brown concluded, "and that God comforted them and gave them serenity of spirit when they went into their last sleep."

Then, as a choir sang softly, the mourners once again moved in quiet unison—down a shady lane to the steps of the Church of St. Sava. Reporters had not received advance copy for the

Two views of miners' graves in the Protestant cemetery.

Ceremony for Greek Orthodox miners at the Church of St. Sava.

Greek Orthodox service, and Ruth Finney wasn't sure what to expect. At the entrance to the church, dressed in black and white robes, Reverend George Kodjich of the Holy Trinity Cathedral of San Francisco waved a censer, and the aroma of its incense lingered intensely on the hot summer breeze. There were no trees here to shade the assembly, as there had been in the other cemeteries, and the crowd squirmed uncomfortably in the scorching sun.

Much of the ceremony was in a language unfamiliar to Finney—she assumed it was Serbian. A small card bearing the eleven names of the Orthodox miners had been distributed to the mourners, and one eventually made its way into Ruth's hands. These were the names that had always been unmistakable in their origin: Begovich, Janovich, Marinovich, Stanicich, Vujovich, and six other miners who had come to America from the war-torn Balkans.

As the bells of St. Sava knelled a final tribute, the somber crowd slowly dispersed and Ruth Finney ambled vacuously back down Main Street to the National Hotel. Her seemingly eternal enthusiasm that had been fed by the nonstop drama of the past three weeks was now thoroughly vanquished by the morning's solemn proceedings.

"Miss Finney," the hotel desk clerk called out to her as she entered the lobby. "I have some mail for you."

She took the small stack of papers from the clerk with disinterest and walked up the stairs to her room. She removed her shoes and hat, poured herself a large glass of water from the pitcher on the bedside table, then picked up the top square of yellow paper—a telegram. It took a couple of seconds for her tired eyes to focus on the pale purple type.

Ruth Finney, National Hotel, Jackson

Your resurrection story widely acclaimed. Mail pouring in from all sections. Pay raised to $50 wk. UP sending check for services. Congratulations.

Matson, Star

Her face brightened slightly, and she reached for the small envelope that was next in order on the stack and tore it open.

Miss Ruth Finney, Sacramento Star, C/O National Hotel, Jackson

Just got to take a couple of minutes this afternoon to comment on your "requiem." I consider it one of those rare newspaper classics. It had everything. Doubtless it was the finest thing of the disaster. I've read it a dozen times. Congratulations—"you're a better man than I, Gunga Din."

Sincerely, Gene Cohn, NEA Service, San Francisco

The Argonaut Mine is clearly visible on the distant hill as last rites are given to miners of the Catholic faith.

The next letter was from Eugene MacLean, president of the *San Francisco Daily News*. As she pulled the letter from its envelope, a check fell out and fluttered to the floor.

Dear Ruth,

Your story "they are not dead but are risen" was the best piece of copy coming out of the Argonaut disaster. Everybody down here agrees. I suppose you know of the bunch of letters and messages the United Press has received. The increase in pay from the Daily News is a slight expression of our appreciation of your work.

E. MacLean, Editor and President, Daily News, S.F.

Ruth picked up the check and for the first time that day she smiled. The amount was $15. With typical Ruth Finney sarcasm, she would later write in her diary, "Riches, at last, from the gold country!"

CHAPTER 13

Pointing Fingers

The long, terrible wait was over—for everyone except Ruth Fessel. In her little one-room shack not far from the headframe of the Argonaut, she continued the vigil. There was no doubt in her mind that her husband had helped to secure the other miners behind the bulkhead on that fateful night, then made his way up the shaft in an effort to open ventilation doors on the higher levels and short-circuit the flow of deadly carbon monoxide.

"He was just that kind of a man," she told reporters. "He would never sit down and die."

Time and again, crews combed the spaghetti-like network of drifts, raises, and stopes above and below the Argonaut 4350 level. Finally, on Sunday, September 23, Byron Pickard put an end to the endeavor.

"A thorough search of the mine has been made," he reported, "but without any discovery of the forty-seventh body. It is now believed that if it is to be found at all, it will be in the water below the 4500 level."

When the coroner's inquest began on Monday, September 25, Amador County's district attorney, T. G. Negrich, knew that taking a hard line against the Argonaut Mine could cost him the upcoming election. He also knew that the heads of various mining corporations, thousands of mining employees in California and throughout the nation, and the eyes of the world would be carefully watching as the investigation progressed.

"One of the most important inquisitions ever held in this state begins today," he told the press. "It is a demand of humanity and the mining industry that a searching inquiry be made. . . . Was the law satisfied? The mere naming of a hole in the ground as an exit does not make it such."

While Negrich could not sidestep the obvious culpability of the Argonaut's owners and management, he planned to redirect much of the blame to those who were charged with enforcing California's existing mine safety orders. "There is no need for more laws. Laws do not prevent disasters unless they are obeyed. The law applicable to mine exits is brief and clear—it cannot be improved upon. With the enforcement of present laws, no new ones are necessary. Unwarranted or unwise mine legislation will spell the end of several counties in this state."

Amador County's DA had set the stage for what was to be a long and complex investigation of the Argonaut Mine disaster. It would begin with a small-town inquest and extend through elaborate probes by federal and state committees. In every instance, the participants understood what Negrich had intimated—laying the blame for the death of these forty-seven men directly on the mine or its management could have a devastating effect on untold thousands whose lives depended on the mining industry.

As director of the inquest, Amador County coroner Delores Potter would also be under public scrutiny. It had not been Potter's goal in life to become a coroner, but it may have been her destiny. When her husband passed away unexpectedly in 1917, she served out his term as county coroner and was officially elected to the position the following year. The cases she had

An unknown miner's son poses at his father's graveside.

investigated in four years were varied and challenging, and they included a number of deaths due to mining accidents. She had already received high accolades from her big-city peers for the way she handled the postmortem examination and identification of the victims. Working together with attorney W. H. Pillsbury of the Industrial Accident Commission, Potter and Negrich would compile a list of eighteen witnesses whom they believed would provide key evidence related to the circumstances surrounding the deaths of the Argonaut miners.

As the primary interrogator, District Attorney Negrich would concentrate on the key questions that had already been brought to light by the press: Was the Argonaut in full compliance with IAC mine safety orders? What was the likely cause of the fire? Was every effort made to rescue the miners?

It would be easy to lay the blame on Clarence Bradshaw for not taking charge and ordering the skips to be sent down in an effort to rescue the men immediately after his discovery of the fire. It would be just as easy to lay the blame on Superintendent Garbarini for not shutting off or reversing the fan immediately upon his arrival at the mine. But Negrich knew that the prominent Amador County businessmen who had been chosen to sit on the Coroner's Jury would not take kindly to such tactics. He was prepared to walk a fine line between aggressive interrogation and artful diplomacy.

When Clarence Bradshaw took the stand on September 25, reporters noted that he seemed remarkably cool for a man who had secluded himself in his home since the early days of the tragedy. For three weeks, he had avoided all contact with the press and the community. But on this day, as he began answering Negrich's questions, newspapers across the country were preparing to run an article purportedly written by Bradshaw exclusively for United Press under the headline "We Did All We Could So Help Me God."

"I would gladly have been one of the men lowered into their grave in Jackson Thursday if I could have saved the life of only one of the men who died in the Argonaut Mine," he claimed. "If my own family had been at the bottom of the shaft, I would have done no more than I did."

The remainder of the article, occupying nearly a full column of the *Stockton Daily Evening Record,* among other newspapers, was nearly an exact duplicate of the statement he would read into the record at the coroner's inquest—a concise and carefully practiced synopsis of the events of August 27.

Clarence Bradshaw photographed in happier days. This photo of the beleaguered shift boss was the only image available to most newspapers.

Negrich finished his interrogation of Clarence Bradshaw with a line of questioning that would become familiar throughout the inquest:

"At any time after you and Pasalich had reached the surface of the mine and had conferred with Mr. Sanguinetti, was it proposed by any person the skips be sent down to the bottom with the idea that the men might get on and come up?"

"Not to my recollection," Bradshaw replied.

"Was it proposed by any person at any meeting at any time that something should be done to get the men out, rather than put the fire out?"

"I don't think so," Bradshaw answered.

"The paramount idea was to fight the fire?"

"Yes," Bradshaw answered. "That was my idea."

*   *   *

In order to accommodate a substantial throng of onlookers, the coroner's inquest was held in Jackson's Love's Hall, normally a venue for minstrel shows, band concerts, and Saturday night dances. By the second day of the inquiry, the audience had heard very little that had not already been hashed and rehashed a dozen times in the newspapers. Thus far, all of the men who had witnessed the fire in the Argonaut shaft during its first hours had testified that it was burning too severely to permit the skips to be sent down in an effort to rescue the miners. The Argonaut skip tender's helper, Mitchell Jogo, would be the first to disagree with that assumption—and the first to imply that a different course of action could have resulted in the rescue of at least some of the trapped men. In the days before the inquest, Jogo had been quite vocal in criticizing the methods used by the Argonaut management on the night of the fire.

There was no doubt that Jogo was the one man who had the best opportunity to view the effects of the fire during its early stages. And now he would give testimony in direct contradiction to that given earlier by Clarence Bradshaw and Steven Pasalich, who he accompanied through the fire zone that night and who left him hanging from the manway ladder just yards above the flames.

"Are you working for the Argonaut now?" Negrich asked Jogo. "Were you fired? Did you say you got fired?"

"I work in the Kennedy over there to get through to the Argonaut," Jogo replied. "I work a couple days. One day it was hot and I was sick and I was in station and tell boss and he tell me to go on top."

"You were fired because you got sick and couldn't work. Is that it?"

"I come to Argonaut and change my clothes. I meet him and he said not come anymore. I said, 'All right, you put my time in office.' He say, 'All right.'"

After several minutes of testimony reviewing his movements on the night of the fire, Negrich began to question Jogo
about the condition of the shaft:

"When you came through the fire, did you get burned—or
anyone else?"

"No, only thing smoke."

"Were the rails bent or crooked?"

"No."

"Straight?"

"Yes."

"Do you think a skip could go down there two or three
times, if you sent it right away?"

"Three or four times it go through—I am sure."

"You looked at the fire for ten minutes?"

"Yes."

"You didn't hear anybody talk about sending the skip back
down to the men?"

"I never heard about it."

"That is all you have to say about the case?"

"Only thing to save the men if skip run down a couple of
times—maybe lose some, but no lose all. Sure it would have
saved some."

The question of whether the miners could have been rescued
during the time that elapsed between the discovery of the fire
and the loss of the telephone and signal bells was best answered
by hoistman Tom Brewer. Coroner Delores Potter questioned
Brewer at length about the speed of the hoisting system:

"How long does it take that skip to go from the collar of
the shaft down to the bottom of the mine?" she asked.

"When I am running full speed, about—I would say between
six and seven minutes."

"Does it take any longer to hoist than to lower?"

"No, the same thing."

"Did anyone at any time . . . suggest that the skips be sent to the bottom in the hope that the men would be waiting for it, owing to their knowledge of the fire, and get on it and come up?"

"Nobody said anything about sending the skip down."

"I have something to say directly," Brewer interjected. "There was no one told me to hold the skip above the fire. . . . I made one suggestion about sending it down or trying to see if it would go through or not. . . . I called the foreman. I asked him what about sending the skip down, and he said then—I think he said it was too late, or words to that effect."

"Suppose you had dropped the skip to the 4800 as soon as you heard of the fire and that the signals had gone off—would it have been possible under these circumstances for the skip to be brought up?" Potter asked.

"I am doubtful, because when my bells went out, it seemed to me that there was something big that dropped down and cut them bell lines and caused the short."

"Were you able to tell from the way the bells went out whether it was something in the nature of a cave-in or merely a timber?"

"It seemed to me it was a big timber that fell across the shaft."

"Would that be likely to stop the skips?"

"I would say it would."

Potter's and Negrich's questioning of Argonaut superintendent Garbarini centered almost entirely on the operation of the Muldoon fan. Negrich formulated his questions to give Garbarini every opportunity to explain and support his contention that reversing the fan would have been detrimental to the trapped miners.

When asked about the lack of fire extinguishers and other firefighting equipment, Garbarini made it clear that the mine did not expect to need such apparatus. Under interrogation by IAC lawyer Pillsbury, Garbarini also implied that the reason Steve Pasalich was unable to get the fire extinguishers to work on the night of the fire was most likely due to his inability to perform the simple operation of that apparatus.

"You recall Mr. Pasalich's testimony that the extinguisher would not work?" Pillsbury asked.

"Yes I recall it. Probably throwing it over—probably the cork might have been stuck. Probably by jerking it a second time. I cannot testify for anything down there, but there's those chances. Probably in the hands of some they will work better than in the hands of others."

Garbarini's testimony concerning the possibility of sending down the skips to rescue the men in the early hours of the fire was carefully worded to support the contention that there was not enough time.

"Can you give an estimate as to how many minutes it would have been possible to get the skips to the bottom and back after the fire was first discovered?" Pillsbury asked.

"It would not have taken more or less than the speed of that hoist—generally between six and seven minutes," Garbarini answered.

"Can you give an estimate of the condition—as to how long the shaft would have remained open for the skips to go up and down?"

"I don't think it would remain open more than half or three-quarters or less than an hour."

"Less than an hour from the time Bradshaw first noticed the smoke?"

"Yes."

"Suppose one or both skips had been sent to the bottom immediately after he arrived on top—would there have been sufficient time to fill them with men and get them up?"

"It is a question, because there were no signals. You would not know when it was time to pull. The engineer would know to go to any station, but they would not know just when to pull the skip or whether there was anyone on or no one at all."

"Can you make an estimate as to how many trips could have been made to the bottom and back after Bradshaw arrived, before the shaft became impassable?"

"Not one trip."

"Why not?"

"On account of the rails buckling and the obstruction in the shaft."

Pillsbury ended his examination with a direct question concerning the allegations made by Mitchell Jogo that the shaft remained open for more than enough time to send down the skips. "Can you reconcile the views expressed by Brewer and Jogo—Mr. Brewer believing the timber fell across the shaft when the signals went out, and Jogo that he watched the fire ten minutes and the timbers had not fallen?"

"Mr. Brewer had evidence of that from the bells being shorted, and this other man—it was only his opinion just how things existed there," Garbarini answered sharply.

"If things were as he described at the time he saw them, would that make it certain that the shaft was still open when the bells went out?" Pillsbury asked.

"That's a question" was Garbarini's curt reply.

District Attorney Negrich saved his most aggressive questioning for the man who in his estimation best represented the ultimate scapegoat for the death of the forty-seven miners, Hugh Wolfin, superintendent of safety for the Industrial Accident Commission. Negrich would attempt to show that the IAC failed to assure that the Argonaut Mine complied with existing mine safety orders and that the deaths of the forty-seven men could have been prevented if the IAC had performed their duties as set forth in those orders.

"Mr. Wolfin, has the commission or any department declared that there was a serious fire hazard at the Argonaut Mine?"

"I believe not."

"You knew of the fire of 1919 in the Argonaut?"

"Yes."

"What is the excuse why a declaration of that kind was not made following the fire?"

"The fire conditions—the fire hazards, rather—at many of the mines are greater than those in the Argonaut, and any such action of the commission would have affected quite a large number of mines. When the mine safety orders were revised, an order was included covering the maintenance of mine rescue equipment or otherwise spoken of as artificial breathing apparatus. There was a serious objection to the order, and finally it became necessary for the commission to accept a substitute in order to secure the cooperation of the mining companies. They showed considerable opposition to elaborate fire protection, and in order to secure cooperation from the companies to prevent mining accidents, the change or special exemption of the commission was granted covering this point of mine rescue equipment."

After several minutes of interrogation on the viability of the Muldoon as an emergency exit, Negrich began to question Wolfin on his credentials.

"Have you ever worked in a mine as a miner?"

"Yes."

"In what capacity?"

"I worked as a miner in Arizona for a few months."

"Therefore, you are not qualified to judge the general character of mining men who are actual miners?"

"Perhaps not, though I have been thrown in with them during my work considerably."

"You have not been in contact with them to enable you to determine the average intelligence or mentality of the average miner, taking into consideration the number that are foreigners?"

"I had thought that I understood them fairly well, Mr. Negrich."

"Have you ever been placed in a position where you could realize for yourself the feeling, the mental status, and the predicament felt by a miner 4800 feet under the surface of the earth?"

"Well, I have been down to that depth a number of times, and on one occasion, when doing mine rescue work, was trapped for a couple of hours, so I think I know something about the feeling that a man trapped would have."

"That was on one occasion?"

"Yes."

"Have you ever allowed it to run through your mind what it meant to a miner to work as deep as 4800 feet in depth under the surface each day that he is able to work, making his case different from the man who occasionally goes down into the mine to inspect or as the result of an accident?"

"I'm not sure I understand. Yes, I have thought of that a number of times."

Obviously feeling that he had pressed the line of questioning to its limit, Negrich returned to an analysis of the Muldoon shaft as a second exit. By virtue of its use as a ventilation draw, it was Wolfin's assertion that the Muldoon would logically cease to be a viable second exit in the case of a mine fire, because smoke and gases would immediately fill the shaft.

"It could be used by men as long as conditions remained normal," Wolfin contended. "But when you have a very unusual condition such as developed here, it could not be used as an exit any more than the Argonaut shaft could be used."

"Then there was no exit," Negrich reiterated.

"Not at that time, no."

"It is also true that a mine with five exits entrapped and took the lives of miners?"

"Yes."

"Then all the legislation in the world will not prevent accidents in mines?"

"Legislation without cooperation will not help it."

"And it is absolutely impossible for mining regulations to overcome the dangers attached to mining?"

"They cannot be 100 percent effective."

"And the Industrial Accident Commission has the power to make such orders and rules?"

"Such *reasonable* safety orders. Any of those orders must be reasonable to be effective."

"If you can point out any way by which a man 4800 feet underground could be protected, would that not be reasonable?"

"The men underground are deserving of all the protection you can give them, but if you require devices that are so expensive that the mines cannot operate, then you will have no men there to protect."

Wolfin was no doubt greatly relieved when Negrich turned the questioning over to Pillsbury of the IAC, whose blatantly leading questions helped clarify the commission's stand.

"Along the lines just discussed by Mr. Negrich, Mr. Wolfin, doesn't the situation come about to this: that before a big accident of this sort happens, the best that any safety institution can do, as for instance the safety department of the commission, is to anticipate and guard against the most likely causes of disaster?"

"That is true."

"It is not possible to make any regulations or any set of regulations that will absolutely prevent all disaster?"

"Impossible."

"To what extent is the cooperation of the mine owners essential to secure safety? Could the Industrial Accident Commission make a large number of stringent regulations that would be received with hostility and then in any way reasonably within its power see that it is lived up to?"

"No. We do not have the men, nor the money to hire the men, to enforce safety requirements that are so drastic that they meet the concerted opposition of the mine operators."

"And any requirement which, if passed, would have put out of business mines running on a narrow margin—would it have met with a great deal of opposition by the mining industry?"

"Yes."

Finally, Pillsbury put to rest the question of the Muldoon as a second exit.

"Do you regard the exit as it now stands as being sufficient to avoid prosecution under the statute where it requires a second exit but does not state for skips to be run through?"

"That is a question for an attorney rather than an engineer. Yes, under existing state law and safety regulations."

"Is it not a fact that there is no penalty provided for the second exit law?"

"No penalty."

"Taking the present disaster, if there had been a cave-in in the Argonaut but no fire, would the Muldoon shaft have permitted rescue of the men?"

"Certainly."

"If there had been a crippling of the hoisting appliances, could they have saved their lives through the Muldoon?"

"Certainly."

"If the fire had started in and about the Muldoon shaft or upcast near there, could the men have gotten out?"

"Almost surely, as they were on the occasion of the last fire."

"Can you adequately ventilate a mine from one shaft, saving the other for an exit?"

"You cannot ventilate a mine by one shaft where they are working spread out as in most of the mines."

"So it is found necessary to use the shaft for ventilation purposes. Do you consider it possible to have put through a law amending this?"

"It would have been impossible."

The testimony of Dr. Lionel Duschak affirmed the uselessness of the Muldoon shaft as an emergency exit or avenue of rescue. On September 5, Duschak had accompanied a crew through the Argonaut 2400 drift to its connection with the Muldoon shaft.

"Were you equipped with apparatus to enable you to go down?" Coroner Potter asked.

"Yes, I wore the oxygen breathing apparatus and went with a regular rescue crew."

"A man without apparatus could not have gone down there?"

"It would have been dangerous to venture down the Argonaut, and fatal to have reached the Muldoon."

"At any time . . . between August 29 and September 5, would it have been possible for a human being to ascend through the Muldoon Mine and its connections?"

"I can only answer by stating that the gases I analyzed at the fan during all of that interval would have been fatal at any time I tested it."

District Attorney Negrich put the question of how the fire might have started to nearly every witness, and not one would express an opinion as to the cause. The Argonaut Mining Company's vice president, Ernest Stent, however, had already made his opinion known through the press.

"The fact that the fire gained such rapid headway leads me to believe that it was the work of incendiaries," he told reporters. "The natural conditions in the mine were not such as to cause sudden bursts of flame. If the fire had started accidentally, surely it would have been detected before it progressed beyond ability to control."

Stent discounted the theory that the fire might have been started by a carelessly tossed cigarette. "Ten thousand cigarettes could not have caused flames to burst forth suddenly, cutting off escape of the miners who were entombed," he declared.

At the end of testimony on September 26, the jurors who had been summoned to inquire into the cause of death for the forty-six Argonaut miners needed very little time to arrive at a conclusion that "they, and each of them, did come to death on the 28th day of August, 1922, in this County by 'Suffocation' from poisonous gas fumes caused by a fire of unknown origin near the 3000 level in the Main Shaft of the Argonaut Mine after they bulkheaded themselves in on the 4350 crosscut, having no means of escape which were free from poison gas."

The question of how the miners met their deaths had been officially answered. The debate over why they died was just beginning.

CHAPTER 14

The Cause
and the Cost

Hailed at first as the fallen hero of the Argonaut tragedy, William Fessel had become the prime suspect in the supposed torching of the Argonaut Mine. On the same day that Fessel's empty coffin was being interred alongside his comrades, Amador County sheriff George Lucot received notification that a person meeting Fessel's description had been sighted in the northern California mining town of Grass Valley. It would be the first of many such alleged sightings.

Through a cooperative effort of the office of the governor of California and the San Francisco chief of police, a notice was sent to law enforcement officials in mining communities through-out the West to be on the lookout for the missing Argonaut miner.

Gentlemen:

I am asking your assistance to locate if possible one Edward William Fessel, who always used the name of William Fessel. The following is his description:

Age, about 40 years; weight about 140 lbs.; height 5 feet 7 inches; blue eyes; fair complexion; light brown hair; almost bald headed; nativity Germany; teeth in bad shape; two out in front upper jaw; occupation miner; drinks considerably; smokes cigarettes, rolls them himself with brown paper and uses Durham tobacco; good education; well versed in chemistry and mathematics; speaks good English and German. He is married and his wife's maiden name was Ruth Liversedge and she is now living with her parents at Pine Grove, Amador County, California, and has a boy about fourteen years of age.

At the time of the fire in the Argonaut Mine (Jackson, Amador County, California), in which forty-six men lost their lives (47 men checked into the mine including Fessel), an inscription was burned on one of the timbers by Fessel, which inscription read, "Gas getting bad," and apparently Fessel tried to fix the time of day. But on the mine being opened after the fire, forty-six bodies were recovered and the body of Fessel to date has not been found, although the mine has been thoroughly explored. It is considerable of a mystery as to what became of Fessel and there is a possibility that he may have escaped from the mine at the time of the fire and for that reason in order to complete the investigation, [knowledge of] his present whereabouts are very desirable, so that a story can be had from him as to how he managed to leave the mine after burning this inscription on one of the timbers.

Would you kindly cause inquiry to be made among all miners and employment agents for the purpose of locating him? If Fessel is alive, there is no doubt but that he will try to secure employment in some capacity about a mining camp or possibly in a lumber camp adjacent to mining camps. . . . The matter is to be treated

entirely confidential and any information you may receive should be transmitted to this Department and
marked "Confidential." In case Fessel is located, contact me immediately and you will receive proper instructions in the matter.

Trusting you will give this your closest attention, I
remain,

Very Respectfully Yours,
D. J. O'Brien, Chief of Police

Chief O'Brien also contacted postal inspectors with the
U.S. Mail service in order to put a watch on incoming and outgoing correspondence from the residence of Mrs. Fessel and
other relatives and friends of William Fessel.

Fessel's background was not that of a typical miner. He
came to the United States from Germany in 1900 and worked
as an interpreter for the U.S. government for a year before moving to Volcano, California, near Jackson, in 1901. For the next
four years, he worked as a forest ranger in California's El
Dorado National Forest. Finally, he settled in Jackson, working
first at the Kennedy Mine, then relocating to the Argonaut
Mine about a year prior to the disaster. Fessel apparently had
no experience in mining before arriving in Jackson, and both
the working conditions and rate of pay for miners was far less
than that of his previous professions.

During the post–World War I era, it was not unusual for
those of German ancestry to receive a cold shoulder from
Americans and others who fought against Germany in the war.
It was also known that German immigrants were generally
anti-Prohibition, and a large number of them were involved in
bootlegging. Despite a general mistrust of Germans among the
miners, Fessel was accepted by his coworkers and well liked—
perhaps even admired—by many of them. The fact that he had

been in America for more than twenty years was, no doubt, in his favor.

William Fessel's wife, Ruth, was the sister of Harry Liversedge, later to rise to fame as General "Whitehorse" Liversedge, commander of the U.S. forces that captured Iwo Jima in World War II.

George Downing, assistant manager of the Argonaut Mine, described Fessel as a "bunkhouse miner." "He used to put in his shift at the mine and go downtown and mine it all over again," Downing told investigators. "He would stand on the street corner and talk about everything. He associated with the general run of men you will find in Jackson on the street corners and on the street and in the soft-drink places. He used to make his headquarters in several of the soft-drink places there in town. . . . As far as I know, he was always a decent sort of chap."

The management of the Argonaut continued to predict that Fessel's body would eventually be found in the mine. Not one Argonaut employee ever intimated (at least publicly) that Fessel was responsible for the Argonaut fire.

When mining engineer William Loring returned to his San Francisco office after attending the Argonaut miners' funerals, a telegram from the governor of California was waiting:

> Mr. Loring,
>
> I have named you one of a special committee of three to investigate into all the facts and conditions surrounding the recent disaster at the Argonaut Mine. The other members of the committee are A. B. C. Dohrmann, San Francisco, Chairman, and John C. Williams, practical miner of long experience, Grass Valley. I have

requested Chairman Dohrmann to begin investigation immediately. He will undoubtedly communicate with you today.

William D. Stephens
Governor of the State of California

Of the three men appointed by Governor Stephens, Loring was most familiar with the manner of operation of California gold mines such as the Argonaut and Kennedy. He was present in Jackson throughout most of the days of the disaster and had participated in many of the executive committee meetings.

A highly respected and successful mine operator, Loring once managed Herbert Hoover's Sons of Gwalia gold mine in Leonore, Australia, and was a good friend of the future president. (At the time of the Argonaut disaster, in 1922, Hoover was serving as secretary of commerce under President Harding.) Loring's expansive Plymouth Consolidated and Carson Hill gold mining ventures were among the most productive in California, due in great part to his broad mining experience and well-honed engineering expertise.

After a short stay in San Francisco, Loring had planned to return to his company's Boston headquarters, but he postponed the trip east in order to devote his full attention to the activities of the governor's committee. He arranged a private meeting with Governor Stephens, who clarified the purpose of the committee and pledged the full cooperation of all state agencies. Loring then rented an office and conference rooms for the group in the Sharon Building in San Francisco. (The committee would later have problems getting reimbursed by the controller at the Industrial Accident Commission, into whose budget they had been integrated.) Although San Francisco businessman A. B. C. Dohrmann would chair the committee's meetings, Loring would do most of the legwork, and the bulk of related correspondence would come from Loring's office.

The governor's committee on the Argonaut Mine disaster held their first meeting on Tuesday, September 29. In the weeks that followed, they would conduct ten private sessions and four public hearings during which forty-three witnesses would provide 347 pages of testimony transcribed from numerous Dictaphone recordings. The committee's objectives were clearly outlined by the governor, and the three men would not stray from their goal "to ascertain the cause of the fire and make such recommendations as the committee would consider to be proper to guard against such disasters in the future."

The owners and management of the Argonaut Mine were now of one voice. They believed that someone had set the fire that entombed the forty-seven miners. They pointed out that there had been no trouble with the electric lines on the night of the fire and that no signs of short circuits or grounding were found. They suggested that the fire had spread much more rapidly than would normally be expected when such a blaze was caused by a candle, match, or electrical short. When the night shift went down at 10:30 P.M., there were no signs of smoke or fire, yet one hour later the fire was burning fiercely across two sets of timbers. Additionally, the Argonaut's own investigation of the 1919 fire at the mine resulted in a conclusion that the fire had been "set by an unknown person or persons."

Argonaut representatives suggested that the fire might have been the work of the Industrial Workers of the World (IWW), a highly radical organization whose members believed that through industrial unionism workers could "secure control of production and establish industrial democracy." IWW members, called Wobblies, were frequently jailed as the result of excessive enthusiasm for their cause. In 1918, federal authorities raided IWW headquarters, charging leaders of the organization with violations of the Espionage Act. A number of suspicious mine fires that occurred prior to the Argonaut disaster were believed to have been set by Wobblies. (In his series for the *Sacramento Star,* reporter Irving Moore's mention of a self-proclaimed Wobbly living in a Jackson Gate boardinghouse no doubt bolstered suspicions that members of the militant organization were in Jackson.)

Even if the science of forensic investigation had not been decades in the future, the area of the Argonaut main shaft where the fire started had been thoroughly destroyed, leaving no trace of causal evidence. Accordingly, the committee's investigation into the cause of the fire depended entirely on circumstantial evidence and expert testimony.

The three men who were the first to pass through the fire zone all testified that the fire appeared to have started in the manway portion of the shaft. The manway contained 2400-volt electric wiring, and a junction box was located in the area where the fire began. Mine workers testified that there had been an electrical short in a junction box at an earlier date that sparked a smoldering fire on the wooden timber to which it was attached. Two Argonaut crewmen who changed out timbers earlier in the day in the area where the fire started testified that their work would not have affected the electrical system, and they had not noticed any problems with the wiring or the box. Argonaut electrician Jack Rule explained that any problems in the electrical system would have thrown the circuit breaker, as it did in the earlier occasion of a short in the junction box.

In testimony before both the governor's committee and the Amador County coroner's jury, Steve Pasalich stated that he rang for the skip on his way to pass out lunch buckets on the night of the fire but nothing happened, so he called Brewer, the hoistman, to see what the problem was. Brewer said that there was a problem with the cable and that he would send down the skip momentarily. The skip finally arrived a few minutes later, and Pasalich thought nothing more of it.

The committee later questioned miner Louis LaBlanca, who traveled up the Argonaut main shaft in a skip with Gligo Minosovich and another miner at the end of their shift at approximately 10:45 P.M. on the night of the fire. LaBlanca testified that the skip stopped unexpectedly at the 800 level and that the two men with him got off, saying that something was wrong with the power. Fifteen minutes later, the skip resumed its upward trip with the three men aboard, arriving at the collar of the shaft shortly after 11 P.M.

In an apparent oversight, neither the coroner nor anyone on the governor's committee questioned hoistman Thomas Brewer about the strangely coincidental power failure, and the relevance of the incident was never pursued. Both LaBlanca and Minosovich testified that they did not know the name of the third miner who was with them that night. The third man was later identified as E. Madureri, who left Jackson during the early days of the disaster and had not been seen since. There is no record that Madureri was ever pursued or even questioned about his actions on that night.

A host of mining men testified before the governor's committee that a fire started by a cigarette or candle could not possibly have advanced as quickly as had occurred that night in the Argonaut. The timbers supporting that area of the shaft were 20 inches square and typically would have smoldered for many hours before bursting into flames. None of the miners who passed through the area in the hour before the discovery of the fire smelled smoke or noticed anything out of the ordinary.

Testimony by Ben Sanguinetti bolstered the theory that the fire could not have started through accidental means. "I located a small fire near the 39 one time that was a short of the electric cable," he recalled. "And we immediately smelled that smoke below. And several times, anybody smoking above—smoking a cigar, for instance—why, it would be detected right away. That is the reason I think the fire was set. If it had been a fire caused by a cigarette or lamp, it would not have gotten to such proportion before they reached it."

Sanguinetti also testified that it would take only two or three minutes for smoke to travel from the 3000 to the 4200 level. When Mitchell Jogo left the 4200 to procure a replacement stop board, he smelled no smoke, yet when Pasalich and Bradshaw stepped out onto the station ten minutes later, the entire shaft above them was filled with smoke.

Both Sanguinetti and Argonaut superintendent Garbarini told the committee about a "plant" that was discovered in the mine in September 1919. In order to produce a timed incendiary device, someone had split a wooden stick and stuck a candle into it so that when the candle burned down it would ignite the stick and start a fire. Fortunately, the candle's flame had been blown out by a draft or the candle had simply burned out before it reached the wood. But it was clear from its placement and from the dry wood chips scattered around it that it was planted by someone who wanted to start a fire in the mine.

Sanguinetti also testified that footprints had been found after the fire in an old drainage tunnel running from the mine to a nearby creek bed. Although neither Sanguinetti nor the committee were prepared to attach any significance to the existence of these tracks, they did concede that this tunnel, which intersected the mine's main shaft approximately 180 feet below the collar and more than 2500 feet above the location of the fire, would have provided a convenient alternative exit for anyone not wanting to be seen leaving the mine.

While the committee could not rule out the possibility of arson, they were extremely skeptical of attempts to lay the blame on the missing forty-seventh man. "This theory, while a bare possibility, seems to your committee to be improbable," they told the Governor. "That William Fessel's body is still in the mine and probably will be found when the shaft has been opened, the mine unwatered and thoroughly explored, seems the more likely theory."

In the end, the committee would fail to arrive at a definite cause of the Argonaut fire. "The evidence given regarding the cause of the fire leads to no one definite fact," they wrote in the final report. "The following possibilities have all been taken into consideration: incendiarism, defective electric wiring, and carelessness with cigar or cigarette stub, carbide lamp, or candle. . . . Of the possible causes, the first two, viz. incendiarism or defective electric wiring, seem to be the most acceptable."

The governor's committee was less timid than others had been in their criticism of Clarence Bradshaw and the failure of Argonaut management to shut down the Muldoon fan as early as possible:

> Judging from the evidence, it would appear to the committee that shift boss Bradshaw did not use good judgment under the circumstances, in failing to notify the men at work on the levels below and in the stopes of the fire; that an endeavor should have been made to warn the men of their danger, and that after this warning had been given under the direction of Bradshaw, he then should have proceeded up the shaft and upon failing to find suitable fire-fighting appliances, his next action should have been to proceed to the surface and stop the Muldoon fan. . . .
>
> This Committee feels that a more effective effort might have been made in immediately stopping the Muldoon fan which would, in the opinion of the committee, have quickly reversed the air currents in the mine, causing the main shaft to work as an upcast. . . .
>
> Some of the witnesses have expressed a belief that the skips should have been sent back in an endeavor to bring the men through the fire zone after Bradshaw and

the two men with him came up. While it is doubtful if this procedure would have been effective, still it should have been tried.

. . . [W]e, the committee, wish to state that under the circumstances, considering the very little training received by Bradshaw and his companions, and without instructions as to action being taken in case of a fire in the main shaft, etc., that Bradshaw cannot be severely reprimanded, with this exception, that he should have notified the men working in the various sections of the presence of fire before he and his companions left the bottom of the mine. . . . [T]he Committee strongly recommends that every foreman and shaft boss, as well as certain underground men, shall be thoroughly trained in the preservation of life and property under every conceivable condition that might arise underground.

The committee admonished the Argonaut Mine for its lack of fire protection equipment and training but stopped short of alleging any infraction of mining regulations. During the period 1916 to 1919, they reviewed a cache of correspondence between Hugh Wolfin, then the IAC's chief mine inspector, and N. S. Kelsey, manager of the Argonaut Mine. In a letter dated February 28, 1916, Wolfin listed a number of changes and improvements he believed were necessary, then implored Kelsey to seriously consider the risks of a mine fire:

As this letter is for your eyes alone, I am going to be just as frank as we were in our conversation. On account of the danger from fire and the extreme depth at which you are working, I feel that the hazard to your miners is very great. There are several things that might make it necessary for the men to come out of the mine, such as the power from the hoist being off, an accident in the shaft which might cause a temporary cave, an explosion of powder, or a mine fire. On account of the conditions as outlined, I feel that I would not be doing my duty if I do not insist that you start work on the requirements outlined at once.

Among the requirements outlined was "a second outlet or escapeway from the mine"; also, that "the use of candles underground should be discontinued as soon as possible."

Additional correspondence indicated that Kelsey had attempted to obtain cooperation from the neighboring Kennedy Mine for a plan to provide a safety exit by connecting the two mines but that his proposal was refused. In testimony before the governor's committee, Kennedy president E. C. Hutchinson stated that he remembered no such request coming from the Argonaut. He did say that during a discussion with one of the IAC inspectors, he had stated his opinion that such a connection would be dangerous to both properties, due to the increased possibility of fire spreading from one mine to another.

By 1919, the IAC had accepted the Muldoon shaft as having met the requirement for a second exit from the Argonaut but was still admonishing the Argonaut manager for permitting the use of candles underground. Through the duration of the committee's investigation, two questions were studied and debated above all others: Should the Muldoon fan have been shut down or reversed? Did the Muldoon shaft truly constitute a second exit?

The committee agreed with the majority of the mining engineers and veteran miners who had given testimony that stopping the Muldoon fan after the first hour of the fire would have been unwise because volumes of smoke and carbon monoxide had filled the mine by that time and the men had no doubt already based their actions on an assumption that the circulating system would remain in its usual mode.

Even so, individual members of the governor's committee stated their personal belief that they would have immediately shut down the Muldoon fan had they been in charge at the time of the discovery of the fire, and, at the same time, they would have immediately sent one of the two skips down in an attempt to rescue the men.

As for the viability of the Muldoon as a second exit, Attorney Warren Pillsbury, referee to the coroner's inquest for the Industrial Accident Commission, epitomized the attitude of most of the mining community in his detailed written opinion of September 28, 1922:

> The second exit situation is unsatisfactory but I believe it conforms to such an extent with existing law as to make prosecution of mines with similar exits without prospect of success.
>
> That the law in its present condition does not forbid a shaft of this type is clear from the following factors:
>
> (1) Neither our Commission nor any District Attorney had considered otherwise, or contemplated proceedings to enforce the statute prior to the disaster.
>
> (2) Universal custom among mine operators in California to construct second exits in this matter.
>
> (3) <u>The law contains no penalty for its enforcement.</u> [his underlining].
>
> (4) The law does not state what kind of escapeway is necessary, or define or specify the emergencies which must be guarded against, i.e., it does not prohibit a shaft which would be adequate for most emergencies but may fail upon some contingencies.

In his recommendation for a permanent interconnection between the Argonaut and Kennedy, Pillsbury also called attention to how little may have been learned from the Argonaut fire by certain parties:

I am informed by our engineers that the Kennedy Mine presents as serious a fire and disaster hazard as the Argonaut did before the fire. Contrasted with this I note in the public press in the last few days a statement attributed to the management of the Kennedy Mine that such a disaster cannot possibly happen to them. My advices are that the Kennedy needs such intercommunication as much as the Argonaut.

As the final day of public testimony came to a close, James Lord of the American Federation of Labor adeptly summarized the difficulties of regulating the mining industry and the practical results of sensible regulations:

Do not think you are going to write a perfect code of law as a result of this thing. I do not think you can hardly write a perfect code of any kind of law. The laws have been brought into effect by the helpfulness of the men who really desire to do good and serve the common good. I am sorry to say the laws have been brought into effect not with the help of the men in the mining camp, but in spite of their position of opposition, for they hate to change their minds.

There is no reason why the mining game should require this toll of human life, the accidents and the crippling of men. I say to you that, by and large, as the laws have been passed throughout the world, the average men who were actively engaged in the game, no matter what their former opinion was, do not want to relinquish the laws or rules, or go back to the old game. They find that in addition to the satisfaction of knowing the men under them are safe and sound, that it is economical mining—that they get the best results, and notice the production per man naturally gets better and greater, because the men work under better conditions.

I hope that every man who can be helpful will continue to be interested in this situation until we have a situation that brings the greatest measure of influence in this industry to the prevention of these disasters.

On December 7, 1922, the governor's committee on the Argonaut Mine disaster held their final meeting in committee headquarters in San Francisco. The final draft of the committee's report was signed and sent to the governor's office, along with final billings and related paperwork. W. J. Loring asked that copies of all the committee's files as well as all correspondence and other papers not accompanying the report be sent to his office for safekeeping. The committee then adjourned *sine die*.

As originally requested by the governor, the bulk of the final report contained "recommendations as will tend to further safeguard the workers in mines and prevent disasters of this kind in the future." Suggestions were received from the U.S. Bureau of Mines, the American Mining Congress, the Industrial Accident Commission (through a special conference chaired by W. J. Loring), and ten prominent mining engineers. Additional input would come from the American Federation of Labor and the California Metal and Mineral Producers Association.

The seventeen recommendations contained in the final draft were nothing new and seemed only logical: that mine timbers should be fireproofed or kept damp through the use of sprinklers; that fire doors should be placed in passageways that connect with the emergency exit; that ventilation fans be installed in such a manner as to be reversible; that serviceable fire extinguishers or water taps be provided at each station; that auxiliary compressed air lines be provided in the emergency exit; that neighboring mines maintain an emergency passage between the two; that some sort of alarm system be installed to warn underground workers; that safe haven compartments be installed near working levels of the mine; that signs be installed to direct miners to the emergency exit; that a plan of action be formulated and conveyed to all supervisors; that a map of the mine be maintained at the collar of the shaft and at each station; that daily inspections be conducted by shift bosses and foremen; that top men be trained in emergency response; that no open flame be left unattended; that oxygen breathing apparatus be available; and that the first duty of anyone discovering an underground fire is to notify the working miners. One recommendation seemed to have been authored by the venerable V. S. Garbarini himself:

(10) A sign shall be posted on each surface or underground ventilating fan station: "This fan shall not be stopped or reversed except by authority of the man in charge of the mine."

Recommendations from Fred Lowell and H. M. Wolfin of the IAC, and James Lord of the American Federation of Labor, were included with the report but were not specifically endorsed by the committee. These were (1) that "the Industrial Accident Commission should be provided with sufficient funds to maintain an adequate staff of inspectors to see that the rules and regulations governing mining are thoroughly and properly enforced"; and (2) that "serious consideration should be given to standardizing all laws that have a general application, providing minimum penalties for the deliberate violation, and giving State mine inspectors the unqualified right to stop a portion of, or an entire mine, when in his judgment, safety requires it." Unlike the committee's suggestions, any application of these recommendations would have required legislative action.

Guided by the recommendations listed in the report of the governor's committee, the Industrial Accident Commission produced an amended section to the mine safety orders to become effective March 15, 1923. For the first time, a section entitled "Enforcement of Orders" appeared in the booklet. This section did not, however, provide for penalties or punishment for failure to comply. Instead, Order #1777 gave the mines yet another way of avoiding compliance "where the enforcement of any order would work a hardship or fail to provide adequate protection in any individual mine, or where any order is unnecessary because of absence of hazard."

For those outside the industry, there had always been the assumption that the silver lining of the Argonaut Mine disaster would be enforceable regulations that would improve mine safety, as the popular Western writer, Frederick Bechdolt, expressed in a *New York Times* article in October 1922:

Miners are not demonstrative men as a rule, and the nature of their calling makes them take many things with a quiet fatalism where other men would show considerable feeling. But since the fire and tragedy in the Argonaut's shaft, miners have been using some very ugly language concerning the so-called second exit. It is natural, of course, that they were the first to realize. Now, however, the realization has spread to officials of the Government, who state that California's somewhat futile law on this matter is one of the most stringent in America, and point to the necessity of legislation commanding hoisting machinery. So, after all, there is a little ray of brightness in this gloom. It is quite possible that other lives may get more safeguards in the future than mere vague words.

Yet four years later in his 1926 technical paper, "Lessons from the Fire in the Argonaut Mine," Byron Pickard handled the subject of regulation with kid gloves, illustrating that the deaths of the forty-seven Argonaut miners had changed little in the mining industry:

> No feasible State regulation can cover all conditions of hazard at every mine. Some hazards can not be eliminated except at prohibitive cost. Mine operators and miners must both recognize the risk, and more time and more thought must be given to applying to individual mines the safety recommendations of State officials and of the Bureau of Mines.

Despite the death of forty-seven men in the Argonaut Mine, the government of California had determined that the value of the state's gold mines far exceeded the risk to human life.

CHAPTER 15

A Dynamic Conclusion

Sometime during the first week of October 1922, Maria Leon and her nephew completed their long trip from Spain, arriving at the Union Pacific train station in Stockton, California. Tony and Luis Leon's cousin greeted them at the station and arranged for transportation to Jackson via auto-stage. Despite the world-wide news coverage, Mrs. Leon had somehow managed to travel from Ellis Island to California without learning of the Argonaut disaster.

Ruth Finney later wrote a fictionalized account of the Leons' arrival—her first foray outside of standard news writing. In the short story, "Promised Land," Finney puts herself aboard the stage, riding alongside the driver as they wait for the cousin to give his relatives the dreaded news that husband and father are dead. But the cousin, whom she calls Jim Biandochi, cannot bear to tell them, and the journey becomes nearly unbearable for Finney, who knows the truth perhaps better than anyone. Finally, the stage tops the hill above Jackson. Finney wrote:

> We were passing the Argonaut mine. Jim Biandochi tried
> to keep his eyes turned the other way, but some fasci-

nation too strong for him drew them toward the light back on the hill that marked the platform and the collar of the shaft where forty-seven men had gone down in the skip that last time.

I couldn't help looking either. There was the mine office, turned into Red Cross headquarters during the disaster. There were the steep wooden stairs where they had carried the stretchers with their shapeless white canvas burdens to the mill far above. And there, forty-seven caskets had stood waiting.

The office and the platform were deserted now. The place was bleak and silent in the dusk.

The woman never glanced toward the mine. Her eyes were fixed on the lights of Jackson, below us. She was too excited now to talk. The boy drummed with his feet against the back of the seat because he could not keep still.

Moments later, the stage pulls down Church Street, past the three cemeteries and the long lines of miners' graves, before stopping at the Biandochi house, where his wife is waiting to take the Leons inside and must break the tragic news. Then Finney describes the sorrowful cries coming from within the house as the stage pulls away.

Although it took some time to distribute all of the proceeds of what was originally called the Goodfellows fund, the widows and orphans of the Argonaut miners eventually received significant monetary aid. The Amador County chapter of the American Red Cross collected thousands of dollars in donations during the disaster from a variety of sources worldwide and additional contributions continued to pour in during the year that followed. More than $45,000 was collected through both individual contributions and the fund-raising efforts of various organizations. Compensation was also paid by the Argonaut Mining Company in the form of back pay and bonuses.

Families of the deceased miners also received money from the State Compensation Insurance Fund. Established by the California Legislature in 1913, this agency worked in cooperation with the Industrial Accident Commission to provide insurance to high-risk industries such as mining. The Argonaut Mining Company and most other members of the California Metal and Mineral Producers Association were insured by this fund. The first widow to receive payment from the Compensation Insurance Fund—a check for $4434.90—was Ruth Fessel.

In the weeks and months following the fire, miners from both the Argonaut and Kennedy were engaged to do personal appearances at fund-raisers. Perhaps the most notable of these was an Argonaut Mine relief ball in Los Angeles sponsored by Grauman's Chinese Theater, as described in the *Amador Ledger* newspaper:

> The boys dress in the regular miners outfit and they appear not only at the Grauman theatre but at others, and the various picture studios there. At the Metro Studio where they appeared one afternoon this week, they took in $1400 in ten minutes.

Attired in the same clothes they wore during rescue operations, five of the *36ers* appeared in a parade on Market Street in San Francisco and at fund-raising balls at the Palace, Fairmont, and St. Francis hotels.

It would be December 1923 before a full accounting of relief fund distributions could be given. Of the forty-seven miners who died in the Argonaut Mine disaster, twelve left widows living in the United States and four had wives still in Europe.

In addition, thirty-seven dependent children would be considered for relief funds, as well as a number of dependent parents, sisters, and brothers in both the United States and Europe. Payments were made in "units" of $670, with dependent wives and children receiving one unit each, parents receiving one-half unit each, and sisters and brothers receiving one-quarter unit each. The largest sum went to the family of Peter Cavaglieri: $2680 to a wife and three children living in Molinello, Italy. Eight of the miners had no dependents, or the existence and whereabouts of any dependents could not be determined. Their final paychecks were donated by the Argonaut Mining Company to the Goodfellows fund.

Ostracized by much of the Jackson community and continually hounded by reporters attempting to protract the Argonaut story, Clarence Bradshaw sold his home and moved his family to Stockton in November 1922. Like many of those involved in the Argonaut tragedy, he would never return to mining.

On January 21, 1923, a representative of the Argonaut Mining Company announced that Superintendent V. S. Garbarini had submitted his resignation. Insiders said the resignation was requested by the mine's board of directors because operating costs at the mine had risen sharply under Garbarini's administration. Friends and family believed that Garbarini had become a scapegoat for the disastrous fire and the company's lack of attention to safety. (During testimony at the coroner's inquest and before the governor's committee, the Argonaut's executives continually and vigorously asserted that all details of mine management, including fire protection, were left absolutely in the hands of the superintendent.)

In the years that followed, Virgilio Garbarini opened a gas station in downtown Jackson, did some occasional consulting work, and continued to serve the community as a county super-visor. The failure of his efforts to save the mine and the men haunted him until he passed away in 1931 from complications of heart disease.

In June 1923, the Industrial Accident Commission ordered the Argonaut and Kennedy mines to construct and maintain a per-manent connection on one of the lower levels. By agreement between the two mines, this link would be made by completing the Kennedy 3900 rescue drift, which was abandoned when the 3600 breakthrough was made. The Kennedy 3900 level coin-cided with the 4650 level of the Argonaut. Therefore, the emer-gency exit would be within a reasonable distance from the work-ing levels of both mines. Despite the fact that representatives of both the Kennedy and the Argonaut had argued against such a connection as an infringement on the rights of private property, neither of the mining companies would contest the ruling.

The Argonaut now estimated the total cost of rescue and recovery efforts, compensation to the miners' families, and de-watering and rebuilding the mine's main shaft at a little over $1 million. This was in addition to the loss of mining income for a period of nearly one year.

During the summer of 1923, workers at the Argonaut and Ken-nedy mines were given a raise of fifty cents per day—a lavish (for the period) salary increase of nine percent. Management at both mines stated their desire that the new pay level would "attract a better class of miners."

On June 2, 1923, in the Mormon Temple in Salt Lake City, Etta Nuttall Ely and her four children were sealed by proxy to her late husband. According to her faith, the family of this Argonaut miner was now joined with his spirit for eternity.

When the first anniversary of the Argonaut Mine disaster came along in August 1923, the Argonaut Mine was still struggling to rebuild its main shaft and dewater the lower working levels. On Monday morning, August 27, all work was once again called to a halt, and Jackson businesses closed their doors in honor of the forty-seven lost miners. Once again, services were held at each of the town's cemeteries, and the graves were strewn with flowers. On Tuesday evening, using a 5-inch banner headline, the *San Francisco Examiner* ran a story proclaiming that William Fessel, the elusive forty-seventh Argonaut miner, had been sighted in the California mining town of Susanville.

For over a year, Ben Sanguinetti struggled to put the tragic fire behind him and concentrate on the work of rebuilding the Argonaut Mine. He was under constant pressure from the Industrial Accident Commission to complete the dewatering of the lower levels so that a connection with the Kennedy Mine could be established, and on September 31, 1923, the 4650 level was finally dry enough to permit cleanup work.

As crews struggled to remove massive amounts of sludge and debris from the 4650 station, crew members Andrew Johnson and Chris Balonevich were ordered to inspect the drift as far as they could safely go and report back with details of the conditions. About 400 feet into the drift, they came across an immense pile of debris that had gathered around the top of a raise that connected to the 4800 level below. During the long dewatering process, as water was being pumped from the 4800 sump, drainage from the 4650 level had created a whirlpool that eventually plugged the raise with trash. As Johnson and

Balonevich moved carefully past the pile of charred timbers and splintered wood, they noticed something within the debris—something starkly white against the blackness of the rubble.

Ben Sanguinetti was on the surface at 8 A.M. when he received an urgent message from shift boss Frank Stage asking the foreman to come down to the 4650 station. Johnson and Balonevich led Stage and Sanguinetti back to the raise, where the four men carefully pulled away the debris to reveal the badly decomposed remains of a human corpse. Little more than a skeleton, the body was on its back, lying on some rubble on the floor of the drift, with its legs down the raise, apparently having been sucked in by the draining water. Under Sanguinetti's supervision, the remains were carefully extracted from the debris and wrapped in canvas, then placed on a stretcher and carried to the surface.

There was no question in anyone's mind that this was the body of miner William Fessel, although there was no way of knowing positively if these were truly his remains. Formal identification was carried out through an examination by a local dentist, Carl Schacht, who had briefly examined Fessel's mouth more than seven years earlier. Schacht had never actually performed work on Fessel's teeth, and the dentist kept no formal records. Schacht's identification of the body was based solely on his memory of that simple exam performed seven years in the past.

After giving a detailed description of the shape of the skull and condition of the teeth, Dr. Schacht presented his opinion, with a caveat: "Of course, you know similar conditions exist in thousands of mouths, but taking the physiography, the general outline of the skull, and in connection with the missing teeth, I would say that was Fessel's skull."

Dr. Schacht's identification satisfied District Attorney Negrich and the Amador County coroner's jury, who ruled that miner

William Fessel, like his forty-six comrades, died on August 28, 1922, of "suffocation from poisonous gas fumes" as a result of the Argonaut fire.

Once more, the town, its mines and businesses, closed in respect for the departed. Once more, Reverend William Brown of the Methodist Episcopal church was called upon to perform last rites. With members of the Volcano Masons serving as pall bearers, the body of Edward William Fessel was laid to rest alongside his fellow miners in Jackson's Protestant cemetery.

How or why Fessel came to his death outside the miners' barricade would remain a mystery. Many subscribed to the theory that he was never with the other miners and that his name on the last-message wall was simply an attempt by the trapped miners to inform rescue or recovery crews that Fessel was not among them. Fessel was working on the 4650 level that night, not far from where his body was found over a year later.

In a reluctant interview with local historian Larry Cenotto in 1997, William Fessel's son, Spencer, said that the message on the mine wall looked like it came from his father's hand and that his father's body must have been one of the forty-six removed from behind the barricade. "That was my reason for thinking that it wasn't him on the outside," he said. "Because it looked like his message on the inside. . . . He couldn't be in two places at one time, that's for damn sure."

One theory was too unthinkable to be publicly verbalized, but during questioning at the inquest, District Attorney Negrich intimated what some were wondering.

"Mr. Sanguinetti, during the time that the rescue work was going on and the other miners' bodies were being removed from the lower levels of the mine, out the Kennedy shaft, were you present during these operations?"

"The most of the time."

"Was it or was it not possible for a body to have escaped and fallen into the mine?"

"Absolutely no chance."

"From the care exercised in the way they were strapped to the cages made it impossible, barring wantonness, where some person deliberately threw the body into the sump, made it impossible for a body to have escaped while it was being removed to the surface?"

"Yes."

Leaving her son, Spencer, with friends in Jackson so that he could continue school there, Ruth Fessel moved in with her mother in nearby Pine Grove. She lived the remainder of her life in self-imposed reclusiveness. She refused further interviews with the press, and both she and Spencer went out of their way to avoid anyone who was seeking information about the Argonaut tragedy.

The memory of the widows and orphans of the Argonaut disaster stayed with Benjamin Sanguinetti. After sixteen years of service, he retired from the Argonaut Mine on February 28, 1925—one day after the birth of his first child. He was the last member of the 1922 management team still employed by the mine. At the end of his final shift, he was presented with a gold watch bearing the inscription, "To Ben from the Boys of the Argonaut." This parting gift was paid for entirely by donations from the working miners.

On the morning of September 7, 1928, fire was discovered at the Kennedy Mine in piles of logs that were waiting to be squared for use as timbers. Due to strong winds and despite the efforts of firefighters and mine employees, the fire quickly spread to the nearby sawmill, then to other buildings. By midday, all of the major structures on the Kennedy property, with the exception of the main office building and mill, were engulfed in flames. An ensuing grass fire moved quickly toward Jackson Gate, where a number of homes were threatened.

At the collar of the shaft, the fire burned a large portion of the headframe, severed the hoisting cable, and cut off all underground electricity. Fortunately, the telephone link remained intact long enough for orders to be given for the men to exit through the connection with the Argonaut, which had been cleared and maintained as an emergency exit in compliance with the Industrial Accident Commission's order.

By late Friday evening, a great portion of the Kennedy Mine lay in ruins. At the time of the fire, the Kennedy's old wooden headframe was being replaced by an all-steel structure, which now lay in twisted heaps above the collar of the shaft. The shaft itself received only minor fire damage. Tests taken underground via the Argonaut connection showed that very little smoke or gas entered the mine.

In the days immediately after the fire, crews went about the work of clearing debris and making repairs. The management of the Argonaut Mine offered to help dewater the lower levels of the Kennedy, and a pipe was laid through the connecting drift for that purpose.

Before repair work began at the collar of the Kennedy main shaft, bulkheads were installed in the shaft at various intervals in order to protect workers on the lower levels from falling debris. On September 25, sparks from an acetylene torch fell onto one of the bulkheads and set it ablaze. Smoke was noticed coming through the water pipe at the neighboring Argonaut and the alarm was sounded. Once again, the Kennedy's underground crews were brought out through the Argonaut Mine.

A 1928 surface fire destroyed the Kennedy Mine headframe and many of the nearby buildings.

The fire was quickly extinguished and work resumed the following day.

Despite the extensive damage, the Kennedy Mine was back in business by December 1928, with a new all-steel gallows frame and hoist. The last of the ongoing lawsuits between the Kennedy and Argonaut had been settled earlier that year, and as a result of this most recent fire, a new spirit of cooperation finally existed between the two old nemeses. Both mines would again experience death and tragedy before their closure, but for the first time since 1894, America's two deepest and richest gold mines would operate side-by-side with a degree of harmony.

*   *   *

On October 8, 1942, War Production Board Limitation Order L-208 signaled the demise of productive gold mining in California and compelled the closure of the Argonaut and Kennedy gold mines. The workforce of the mining industry was needed for the war effort, and gold was not considered a strategic war metal.

Attempts to reopen the Argonaut and Kennedy mines after the war were futile. Both mines had filled with water, and three years of neglect had taken their toll on maintenance-dependent shafts and drifts. After a century of productivity, California's two famous gold mining giants had become little more than tourist attractions.

The opportunity to cover the Argonaut Mine disaster provided Ruth Finney with what was quite literally the break of a lifetime. In 1923, Scripps-Howard newspapers transferred her to San Francisco, where they groomed her to become the agency's premier Washington correspondent. Living in a bay-view Sausalito apartment with her mother and writing hard news and feature articles for the *Daily News* and other Scripps-Howard newspapers, she already felt that her new career had taken her far beyond her dreams.

In the fall of 1923, as the *Sacramento Star* offices were being dismantled by the newspaper's new owners, the *Sacramento Bee,* Ruth Finney boarded a train for Washington, D.C. As one of only nine women with Senate gallery credentials, she would provide national political coverage for Scripps-Howard newspapers in California; Albuquerque, New Mexico; Denver, Colorado; and El Paso, Texas. Her work on the Teapot Dome Scandal and the Colorado River dam project, as well as her acclaimed series on the life and times of Eleanor Roosevelt, would bring her national accolades.

In 1929, Ruth married "Washington Merry-Go-Round" guru Robert Sharon Allen. In 1931, she was nominated for a Pulitzer prize for her investigation of corruption in the electric and gas utilities industry. In 1937, she was interviewed by NBC radio in San Francisco and asked to repeat the story of how she scooped more than 100 newsmen at the Argonaut Mine disaster—in the words of radio commentator Jeffrey Baird, a story that had become "something of a journalistic classic here on the coast."

Scripps-Howard took great pride in never having asked Ruth to write a sob-sister article. "We've never asked her to do the woman's angle on a story," said Scripps-Howard editor-in-chief Walker Stone in 1971. "She's far too proficient in too many other things."

Although her name was never as familiar to the public as her nephew, science fiction author Jack Finney, Ruth was highly respected by her peers and became a recognizable icon in the Washington, D.C., inner circle. She was perhaps best known for her "Washington Calling" column, produced from 1941 until 1974, when she was forced into retirement by a progressively worsening eye problem. Ruth Finney passed away in 1979 at the age of 81.

Ironically, Ruth's counterpart at the *Stockton Record,* Pearl Wright, who had always planned a lifelong career as a newswoman, continued to write for the newspaper for several years after the disaster, then faded into obscurity.

By the time Jackson's World War II vets returned home from Europe and the South Pacific, the winding drifts of the Argonaut and Kennedy mines, still rich with gold, had collapsed and filled with groundwater. The cost of mining and milling now

A publicity photo of a more sophisticated Ruth Finney taken in San Francisco by her employer, Scripps-Howard News Service, just one year after her reportorial triumph at the Argonaut Mine disaster.

exceeded the value of the gold, and so it would remain into the next century. Amador County would survive for a time on ranching and the timber industry. Not far from the headframe of the Argonaut Mine, the sprawling complex of a Georgia-Pacific lumberyard employed a significant number of the town's workforce until the plant closed in the 1990s, dealing yet another blow to the local economy.

Today, the laid-back little community—a stark antithesis of its rowdy past—survives on tourism and a close proximity to popular wineries and ski resorts. The town's communal activities still circle primarily around the Italian and Serbian population, almost all of whom have more than a few hard rock miners in their pedigree.

For the most part, the progress of mine safety in the twentieth century is tied directly to coal mine tragedies. State and federal lawmakers nationwide had always paid far more attention to the coal mining industry than to gold mines and other metal-producing mines. In 1940, 257 miners died in coal mining accidents. The following year, Congress passed the Coal Mine and Safety Act. This law granted rights to federal inspectors to make annual inspections of coal mines. Like so many mining laws before it, it provided no enforcement provisions. The law was "strengthened" in 1947 to include a proviso allowing notification to operators guilty of infractions but still no provision of enforcement. The law was once again passively amended in 1951, after the deaths of 119 coal miners in West Frankfort, Illinois.

Finally, in 1969—one year after 78 men perished in a Farmington, West Virginia, coal mine—Congress passed the Federal Coal Mine and Safety Act, which included mandatory fines for violations and criminal penalties in the case of willful neglect. Neither this law nor any other on the books at the time provided compulsory safeguards or enforcement for the safety of men working in gold, silver, copper, and other metal mines.

It would take the deaths of 91 miners in the Sunshine silver mine in Kellogg, Idaho, in May 1972 to bring the plight of non–coal miners to the attention of lawmakers. Still, five more years would pass before a wide-scope mine safety act was passed that placed coal, metal, and nonmetal mines under a single umbrella. The responsibility for enforcing this law fell to the Mine Safety and Health Administration, a then newly created division of the Department of Labor.

Today, the amount of gold mined in the United States is minuscule compared to deep mines of South Africa and other countries. California's few remaining active gold mines struggle to make a profit, and few, if any, are considered legitimate gold producers. Most effective milling processes require the use of chemicals banned under the state's strict environmental protection regulations, and even those that send their ore to less-restrictive Nevada for milling are targeted by environmental activists for littering the landscape with waste rock. For the most part, California's modern gold mines make far more profit from the tourist trade than from the relatively minor amount of ore they unearth.

In 1922, the Argonaut tragedy was the worst mining disaster that had ever occurred in the state of California. Unless the country returns to a gold standard, and, at the same time, there is a drastic change in the way gold is mined and processed, the Argonaut disaster will probably always remain the worst *gold* mining disaster in the history of the United States.

Even though for many decades both the state and federal governments were hesitant to regulate the metal mining industry beyond providing basic safety recommendations, the lessons learned from the Argonaut fire would indirectly help protect the lives of thousands of miners, in all types of mines, across the United States. Unfortunately, the first effective safety legislation combining coal and metal mines was passed thirty-five years after gold mining ceased to be a viable industry in the state of California.

The Forty-Seven

BACHELLER, ELMER LEE—Protestant; age 56; birthplace, California; wife, name unknown; no children. Bacheller was not a regular miner at the Argonaut. He volunteered to work for a friend who went on vacation.

BAGOYE, PETER—a.k.a. Bajoge; Catholic; age 24; birthplace, Austria; wife, name unknown; no children. Bagoye had been in America for only four months. He had previously served in the Austrian Army during World War I and was expecting his wife to join him from Austria soon.

BALDOCCHI, RAFAELO—Catholic; age 29; birthplace, Italy; single.

BEGOVICH, RADE—Greek Orthodox; age 36; birthplace, Yugoslavia; single.

BOLERI, D.—Catholic; age unknown; birthplace, Italy; single.

BUSCAGLIA, EUGENE—Catholic; age 25; birthplace, Italy; wife, Clotilda; no children.

CAMINADA, JOHN—Catholic; age 24; birthplace, Italy; single.

CAVAGLIERI, PETER—Catholic; age 40; birthplace, Italy; wife, Emilia; three children, John, Josephine, and Agrentina.

CLAYTON, JAMES—Protestant; age 36; birthplace, California; engaged to Myrtle Richards. Clayton's two brothers, Charles and Valentine, worked on the rescue crews. His fiancée was the widow of a miner killed in another local mine.

DeLonga, Paul—Catholic; age 31; birthplace, Austria; single.

Ely, Evan—Mormon (interred in Protestant cemetery); age 29; birthplace, Texas; wife, Etta; four children, Bobbie, Hilda May, Eugene, and Emma. Ely's brothers-in-law worked on one of the rescue crews.

Fazzina, A.—Catholic; age 37; birthplace, Italy; single.

Fessel, Edward William—Protestant; age unknown; birthplace, Germany; wife, Ruth; child, Spencer. Fessel was a former chemist in Germany and interpreter for the U.S. government. His wife was the sister of Harry Liversedge, later famous as the commander of conquering forces at Iwo Jima in World War II. As the missing forty-seventh miner and the man whose name appeared on the last-message wall, Fessel would become the biggest mystery of the Argonaut disaster.

Fidele, V.—Catholic; age 38; birthplace, Italy; single.

Fitzgerald, Charles T.—Catholic (interred in the Protestant cemetery alongside his best friend, James Clayton); age 27; birthplace, California; wife, Frances; children, Donald and Janet.

Francisconi, Simone—Catholic; age 48; birthplace, Italy; single.

Gamboni, Battista—Catholic; age 33; birthplace, Switzerland; single.

Garcia, Timothy E.—a.k.a. Enrique Harismendez; Catholic; age 48; birthplace, California; widower; children, Lorenzo and Mary.

Gianetti, Maurice—Catholic; age 44; birthplace, Italy; single.

Giorza, Giuseppe—Catholic; age 36; birthplace, Italy; wife, Virginia; five children, Louis, Mary, Nilda, Annie, and Madelina. The Giorza family lived in a cottage on Kennedy Flat, not far from the mine.

GONZALES, LUCIO—Catholic; age 28; birthplace, Italy; single.

JANOVICH, MARKO—Greek Orthodox; age 35; birthplace, Serbia; wife, Stane; no children.

JOVANOVICH, MILOS—Greek Orthodox; age 36; birthplace, Montenegro; single.

KOSTA, MANUEL—Catholic; age 47; birthplace, Portugal; single.

KOVAC, JEFTO—a.k.a. Kovacevich; Greek Orthodox; age 42; birthplace, Herzegovina; wife, Rista; three children, Jovanka, Novica, and Manojlo.

LAJOVICH, RADE—Greek Orthodox; age 33; birthplace, Montenegro; single. Lajovich had just started working for the Argonaut after returning from military service in World War I.

LEON, ANTONIO—Catholic; age 33; birthplace, Spain; wife, name unknown; three children, names unknown. Antonio Leon's son was en route from Spain with his brother's wife.

LEON, LUIS—Catholic; age 42; birthplace, Spain; wife, Maria; four children, names unknown. Luis Leon's wife was en route from Spain with his brother's son.

MANACHINO, BATTISTA—a.k.a. Maracino; Catholic; age 40; birthplace, Italy; single. August 27 would have been Manachino's last shift at the Argonaut. He planned to return to his former work as a baker.

MARINOVICH, STEVE—age 46; birthplace, Serbia; marital status unknown; four children, names unknown.

MASLESA, JOHN—Greek Orthodox; age 32; birthplace, Herzegovina; single.

MILLER, ERNEST—Protestant; age 37; birthplace, Illinois; wife, Catherine; two children, names unknown. Miller was a survivor of the greatest metal mine tragedy of the early twentieth century at Granite Mountain copper mine, Montana, in 1917, where he was trapped for four days.

MILJANOVICH, TODORE—Greek Orthodox; age 37; birthplace, Herzegovina; single.

O'BERG, ARTHUR WILLIAM—Protestant; age 27; birthplace, Washington; wife, Anna; child, Florence. Son of Charles O'Berg, who also perished in the disaster.

O'BERG, CHARLES—Protestant; age 55; birthplace, Sweden; widower; children, Arthur and Elmer. Charles and Arthur O'Berg arranged their schedules so that they could work together. Charles planned to retire in 1923.

OLIVA, PIO—Catholic; age 25; birthplace, Italy; single. Oliva's brother, Luigi, was a miner on the same shift but had taken the weekend off to visit friends in San Francisco.

OLOBARDI, EMANUEL—Catholic; age 27; birthplace, Italy; wife, Amelia; no children. Before going to work that night, Olobardi told his wife, "I fear something awful is going to happen."

PAVLOVICH, ELIA—Greek Orthodox; age 40; birthplace, Dalmatia; wife, name unknown. Pavlovich's wife was pregnant at the time of the disaster.

PIAGNERI, ALDINO—Catholic; age 27; birthplace, Italy; single.

RUZZU, GIOVANNI—Catholic; age 28; birthplace, Sardinia; single.

SEAMANS, BERT—Protestant; age 38; birthplace, California; single. Seaman's father had been unaware of his son's whereabouts until hearing of the disaster. The father waited on the mine property for many days before giving up hope and returning home.

SIMONDE, DOMENICO—a.k.a. Domenic Simone or Domenic Simmons; Catholic; age 47; birthplace, Italy; single.

STANICICH, NIKO—Greek Orthodox; age 40; birthplace, Serbia; wife, Mary; three children, Mary, George, and Bobby.

STEINMAN, GEORGE L.—Catholic; age 48; birthplace, Michigan; wife, Linda; four children, Harold, George, Lester, and Warren George, an infant. Steinman's pregnant wife told the press that her husband verbalized a feeling of foreboding about going to work that night.

VILLIA, DANIELE—Catholic; age 43; birthplace, Sardinia; single.

VUJOVICH, MIKE—Greek Orthodox; age 28; birthplace, Herzegovina; wife, Maria; two children, names unknown.

ZANARDI, CESARE—a.k.a. Lanardi; Catholic; age 26; birthplace, Italy; single.

Compiled from the Amador County coroner's report, articles in the *Amador Ledger* and *San Francisco Bulletin,* and the records of the Amador County Red Cross. Miners were listed as single when an investigation of their background turned up no record of family. Name spellings are based on research into multiple sources, including information from descendants, but are not necessarily correct in every case.

Bibliography

Allen, Frederick Lewis. *Only Yesterday: An Informal History of the 1920s.* New York: Harper & Bros., 1931.

Amador County History. Edited by Mrs. J. L. Sargent. Jackson, CA: Amador Federation of Women's Clubs, 1927. Reprint by Cenotto Publications, 1977.

Cenotto, Larry. *Logan's Alley: Amador County Yesterdays in Picture and Prose,* volumes 1 and 2. Jackson, CA: Cenotto Publications, 1988.

DeMarchi, Jane. *Historical Mining Disasters.* Beaver, WV: National Mine Health & Safety Academy.

Gentry, Curt. *The Last Days of the Late, Great State of California.* New York: Random House, 1969.

Historical Summary of Mine Disasters in the United States—Volume 3—Metal and Nonmetal Mines—1885–1998. Beaver, WV: National Mine Health & Safety Academy.

Jarvis, C. E. "Report to Governor William D. Stephens on the Argonaut Fire: September 22, 1922."

Mason, J. D. *History of Amador County California.* Oakland, CA: Thompson & West, 1881. Reprint by Cenotto Publications, 1994.

Peele, Robert. *Mining Engineers' Handbook.* New York: John Wiley & Sons, Inc., 1927.

Pickard, Byron O. *Final Report on Argonaut Mine Fire Disaster, 1922.* Berkeley, CA: U.S. Bureau of Mines, 1923.

Pickard, Byron O. *Lessons from the Fire in the Argonaut Mine.* Washington, DC: U.S. Department of Commerce, Bureau of Mines, 1925.

Index

Muldoon shaft (Muldoon Mine),
continued
as ventilation system for
Argonaut Mine, 25–26
Murphy, Lloyd "Doc"
actions on night of fire, 40–41
heads Argonaut rescue crews,
56, 139
heads recovery team, 162

National Hotel, 67, 74, 200
San Francisco *Chronicle* phone
line to, 111–112
nativism, 93–94
NEA, 146
Negrich, T. G.
at coroner's inquest, 202–205
newspapers, 65–66
inaccuracies of, 65, 177
list of Sacramento based, 66
methods described, 62
reporters banned from
Argonaut property, 64–65,
69
reporters banned from Kennedy
property, 115–119

O'Berg, Arthur (son) and Charles
(father), 22, 162, 196, 256
O'Berg, Elmer (son of Arthur),
108
O'Brien, D. J., 220
O'Connell, Father Michael,
194–195
Oliva, Luigi, 96
Oliva, Pio, 96, 194, 256
Olobardi, Amelia, 14
Olobardi, Emanuel, 194, 256
has feeling of foreboding, 14
ore (gold)
extraction from stopes, 5

low grade vs. high grade, 8
mining and milling of, 6
ore cart, operation of, 2

Pacific Telephone, 58
installs exclusive lines for
newspapers, 111–112
Pasalich, Steve
as Argonaut skip tender, 8–11
before governor's committee,
224
interviewed by Pearl Wright, 59
movements on night of fire,
15–16, 22–25, 30–32,
36–37, 41
Pathe Newsreels, 63, 100
Paul device (breathing apparatus),
47
Pavlovich, Elia, 82, 256
Penrose, Thomas, 140
Perovich, Andrew, 13
photographers, 63–64
Piagneri, Aldino, 256
Pickard, Byron O., 51, 104
and body miscount, 182–183
first to enter Argonaut after
breakthrough, 148
in charge of rescue and
recovery, 138
movements on first day of fire,
43–44, 50–54
Pillsbury, Warren H.
opinion on mining laws, 230
represents IAC at inquest, 204
placer gold, 87
plant (arson device), 226
Plymouth (California), 87
Plymouth Consolidated Mines,
222
Portugal, 93
Posey, O. K., 112